Sarah's Tent

Sarah's Tent

Hester Beukes

iUniverse, Inc.
New York Lincoln Shanghai

Sarah's Tent

iUniverse books may be ordered through booksellers or by contacting:

iUniverse
2021 Pine Lake Road, Suite 100
Lincoln, NE 68512
www.iuniverse.com
1-800-Authors (1-800-288-4677)

ISBN: 978-0-595-44435-9 (pbk)
ISBN: 978-0-595-88762-0 (ebk)

Printed in the United States of America

To our Lord Jesus Christ for His
unfailing grace and guidance
I humbly offer my gratitude

He that reads and grows no wiser
Seldom suspects his own deficiency, but
Complains of hard words and obscure sentences,
And asks why books are written
That cannot be understood

Samuel Johnson

Contents

PART THREE SARAH

PART FOUR THE BRIDE

Dear Would-be Reader,

Mr. and Mrs. I-Me-Mine.You have met them, yes? Mr. expects his wife to pamper every ounce of his self-image and pander to every inch of his other interests. Mrs has her world revolving solely around her boutique image and fears the day her bathroom mirror comes to crack. Yesterday they were a couple. Today they are separate names—one more failure added to the listed statistics of failures. This book, however, is written with love to those who would dare try again.

Folk want to read a gripping story right from the first word and I was told I don't seem to have one: the beginning is slow, and puzzling. Step up the action. Re-write this, re-phrase that. You will need to shuffle those and just re-arrange these. Delete, delete. Cut, cut, cut. Yet the number of analysts, who but skimmed, took a good look at, or spent hours with the manuscript, all championed publication of Sarah's Tent. But then of course, it would first have to undergo major surgery—and not much of love is seen either. Add some. Am I not rather harsh and comfortless? So it went on and on.

Well then, think I, the point has been missed. Entirely.

I was furthermore advised to make up my mind about the kind of reader I wanted to reach: the more-intellectuals or the man in the street? This policy is called 'being consumer-friendly.' I then baulked. I am sticking to the man in the street simply because, well, because he is Me. Us. Just ordinary Us. So you are getting Sarah's Tent to read just as I got it to write.

If the book ends with a sigh of contentment, then I now let it begin its journey with a sigh of peace, for I am yielding to an inner prompting urging me to submit for publication without the advocated appeasement I therefore enjoin well-disposed readers, also the cautious ones, to move beyond imperfections. Invite the Holy Spirit to take over and then delight in what He will do for you.

Let us praise God Almighty for His everlasting grace extended usward.

With love, Hester

Cape Town, South Africa
February 2007

FOREWORD

Homo Sapiens! In terms of eternity, and the assumed age of the earth, man appeared on the scene but yesterday—say between a quarter and a half million years ago.

Anthropologists tell us this: roughly 35000 years back he had developed sufficiently to form his first artillery; spearheads of bone and flint, followed by bow and arrow. Then, about 5000 years ago comes his carving and his paintbrush, thus his first system of communication and recording. And there you are—we have gotten us our historians!

But Christians *know* this: 2000 years ago he received the Message of Love and this is the biggest single event in the development of mankind, since creation, with which his Creator could have blessed him.

Now we face several options, and each of these claim many adherents. We may either accept the Book of Genesis (and the whole Bible) verbatim as the inviolate Word of God. Or alternatively, we may question it sensitively, sensibly or foolishly, or we may refute it either partly or totally.

Whatever our inclination, none of these options should stop us from observing the results of human administration. What has Homo Sapiens done with his heritage? Exegetics of Scripture have, swayed by gender even if unwittingly, more than once played a major role in swinging the course of history—popular tenet flows as does the tides of fashion. But the Divine injunction comes clear: let those who are committed to Jesus, come out from amongst them.

We have not anywhere near begun understanding radical Christianity, and neither have we come anywhere near to understanding the radical purposes of God for the elect body of His Son.

We may not have drunk as deeply from the bitter cup of sorrow and utter despair as Jesus did, as much as we know that only firsthand experience of suffering can bring forth the agony of soul Christ exemplified, and asks of us before we can truly forgive as He did. We speak too easily of drinking the dregs for His sake.

Ultimately, God has forgiven us for participating in the evil He created *(Is.45:7 KJV)*. This perfect work of redemption was done through His Son. We see the evils of Sodom and Gomorrah rife in this day as ever it was. It is fast reaching the scale of Biblical prophecy. *Then shall they begin to say to the moun-tains, Fall on us, and to the hills, Cover us (Luk.23:30).*

Israel rejected Yeshua Hamasheach *(Mat.27:25)* and Jerusalem took Him out-side the city walls. We likewise are keeping the Eternal Groom out of our private chambers *(Songs 5:3-6).*

Faced daily with conclusive evidence, together with the stinging reality of dec-adence and destruction on a global scale, and in spite of intellectual feats, man cannot solve the mystery of life and death. He has no access to the knowledge that can save his personal existence on earth, neither has he any hope of gaining access to immortality by developing all his faculties and abilities. The plight in which the world finds itself is gradually beginning to invade his thinking pro-cesses: man has eaten of the fruit of the tree of knowledge of good and evil but he cannot produce everlasting life—the one tree guarded against all his probing. He can never eat of its fruit because it is beyond his unregenerate reach.

Man cannot even manage and develop that which was placed in his care: the remarkable spiritual qualities built into woman to clothe and complete him.

Cynics persist in decrying, and stubbornly resist all thought of the Godhead. They refute the resurrection power of the Father through Christ Jesus and the Holy Spirit to walk freely all his days on planet earth, as was the intention of God for the first man.

The author is convinced that her obdurate resistance and eventual conversion to Jesus Christ represents thousands upon thousands of souls caught in the con-stricting coils of external religion, and who have no hope of release unless there are faithful, nameless, Spirit-led ones answering God's call on their lives to inter-cede for the captive. This is what this book is all about.

The Apostle Paul received as much enlightenment in three days of blindness as most believers do in a lifetime of seeing. May God therefore raise Himself spe-cialized nannies, saintly men and women in the Body, who will answer His call and accordingly provide the new-born babes with appropriate spiritual suste-nance and vital post-natal care.

Inspired by Jeremiah's boldness of speech, further incentive is drawn from my own bitter-sweet well and all timidity and hesitation is set aside as I emphatically declare that where God has fused together the peculiar spirit of a reborn man and a reborn woman, He enjoins them to multiply and produce spiritual progeny for His Kingdom. The church that does not reconsider predisposed doctrinal issues in this respect is not fully in the will of God.

First Adam let his bride take the reproach.

Last Adam so loved His bride He died for her.

But who, then, is the Bride?

I have a burden to speak out. I am, therefore, addressing mainly those couples, married, which have mutually made a commitment to Jesus Christ.

Several aspects in this dissertation apparently divert from the main stream of debate, but converge again to form an urgent exhortation to the Body of Christ. I worked from the older King James Version.

H.B.

PART ONE

RECOGNIZING, RECONSIDERING, RETRIEVING

... taking another look at Genesis

To amplify the purpose of

To carry into effect

Eve
SUB
Woman

Working together with

Executive

An extremely influential
and powerful position that
effectively engineers and,
in fact, delivers the goods

Single
Couple
BRIDE
Body
Church

A particular task

A charge

Adam
MISSION
Man

A purpose

A goal

An assignment to be
completed

A spearhead

1

SPIRIT LIFE OF CALIBRE

Fusion Called For

You are invited to consider the biggest bluff, and certainly the most damaging, that Satan has succeeded in pulling off. Of course, you may throw the arguments raised in the bin if you feel that is where it belongs, but think again you certainly will!

God is separating unto himself husbands and wives who have fused to oneness of mind, and who will seek Him as He had originally intended Adam and Eve to walk with Him. Sadly, the couples willing to walk this Way are few.

However, when a serious and determined couple desire to move into a deeper level of obedience, they are certain to find themselves searching for an understanding of the principle of submission. Additionally, they will find Scripture revealing how the Body is to respond to set-apart couples.

Let it be fully understood that God would have Himself not quantity, but quality—not doing, but being. The focus therefore is not on added membership to a denomination, but on spirit life of calibre.

Do you think it true of New Testament churches today as having the same spiritual impact on the secular world as in the first days of the Book of Acts? Christians are grieved by what is happening world-wide, yet the pace at which God is moving to perfect His end-time plans gladden their hearts. Time is short and the Church is to be found not static but moving in the flow of His workings. It is therefore essential for both Body and saint to rectify or remove all blots and blemishes the Holy Spirit reveals.

The general misconception of 'submission.' can be listed as an impediment.

The very life of the Body and its growth depends on our personal honesty as we beseech God for a spirit of repentance to touch every individual and sweep over this land. Intercession requires single-minded purpose, but do we really have the kind of backbone to bring us into cleaving wholly to our Master and Lord? To boldly and courageously do away with what is redundant?

Behold, thou desirest truth in the inward parts; and in the hidden part thou shalt make me to know wisdom (Ps.51:6).

Therefore, as Christians deeply rooted in the Word, we need to scrutinize and seriously consider every area possibly retarding the progress of our brothers and sisters and we are circumventing the charge laid on the Body if we do not deal effectively with what the Holy Spirit reveals. It takes courage to expose blind spots, and work at them effectively. So strong are the bonds of tradition and legalism for instance, that only resolved probing can dislodge and uproot it.

The Unwilling Bride

In considering possible hindrances, a number of questionable areas come to mind. One such is in-submission, closely related to rebellion. No groom would be interested in an unwilling bride, and to employ an impertinent cliché: what would Jesus (the eternal Groom) do?

At the root of insubmission lies disobedience, parented by ignorance and independence of spirit, and this unruly family always operate in direct opposition to the Rest of God.

Once we recognise the cause of a problem, we should get down to the business of reconsidering, and be willing to follow up with rectifying and retrieving. As always, the truth releases and sets free.

Thus, when a couple comes to understanding and entering the rest of God, they should already have dealt with disabling and interfering influences and, with the gift of discernment operating effectively, ably conduct warfare and hold their fort.

When God joins a man and woman through rebirth (viz. Abraham and Sarah), a Divine project of magnitude is set in motion. Such merging is from His heart and He considers them as coupled and yoked, to live as one, to work and have their being in Him alone, and to produce spiritual progeny. Indeed an awesome state of 'being,' and we will never in this life fully understand the significance and power generated in spiritual fusion. By His Spirit, our Father brings these His elect together, and pours their spirit into the spirit of a many-member Bride for His beloved Son *(Rev.19:7-9, 21:7-11,27, Eph. 4:15,16).*

2

JUST BECAUSE THE BIBLE SAYS

Human Presumption

Bold and controversial statements always invite us to probe and lay aside personal perceptions pro tempore. More than likely your reading of *Genesis Chs. l, 2 and 3* has been influenced by generations of traditional exegesis, but looking at these chapters yet one more time, from a totally different angle, may induce the reader to fresh and fruitful debate.

What is forthwith being imparted calls for brave men who will raise the trumpet and dauntlessly expose the dark deceit restricting the Church in her present walk.

The majority of Christians are sincerely religious. By and large, they are well meaning and unpretentious; many without academic degrees, some quietly denying prestigious fanfare, many never advertising notable qualifications, while others brilliantly peg apathetic washing on their lines, never taking firm stand in meetings, fearing to appear inferior yet feeling and showing it.

Nevertheless, these wholesome, sound, beautiful people rarely boast and they are staunch and reliable in their congregations. They are fixed, established, and settled in their beliefs. They are unshakable Christians and countrymen—sailing vessels becalmed in the middle of their own little pond, content, albeit unwittingly a prey to tradition or fresh (illegal) innovations. How easily unchallenged religiosity becomes an idol!

Sincerely religious? Many are the believers not only accepting verbatim from their shepherds, but also are dependent on the exegesis of countless learned theologians; now and before, who themselves in turn rely on ancient, unnamed script copyists. Side notes included. From the same school of thought, of course?

Now, orthodoxy comes to us straight through the teachings of Jesus and has been captured for us in writing by the Apostles toward the end of the first century. Paul stands out as a contender for the title 'Toughest of 'em All'. But it takes courage for believers to not succumb to side-tracking, letting them-selves be either jostled or stoned out by Current Persuasions. Chronicled archaeological finds, and theories are discarded or approved of by modern technology and grave matters are mostly sorted out, weighed and packaged by the advanced and enlightened ones and then lapped up by the lay. But unless repeatedly proven, why follow suit?

There will always be some who declare their holy scriptures are given through supernaturally, and therefore the only possible truth of God available to man, and so thinking form exclusive sects using their own bible. A veritable Babel of influences … narrow is the way; few indeed finding it …

Should we not rather permit the Jeremiahs of our day to take hold of audacity and state unequivocally when and where there are self-ordained wolves operating and spiritually fleecing the flock with apparently innocuous and conventional religious conversations all done 'in the Name of Jesus Christ, our Lord and Saviour, Amen!' *(Is. 56:10,11)*?

Fortunately for us, God has graciously made provision for presumption: He knows the human heart all too well! Too easily do we accept the insidious whisperings of the Evil One, either nurturing redundant traditions or passing dead works on to the next generation.

Taking The Strong Meat

God is aware of the difficulties those endure who will not toe the line to this world and its convenient religious interpretations and activities, and who desire *to come unto a perfect man, unto the measure of the stature of the fullness of Christ (Eph. 4:13).* There is reward for those who wait on God with the Word Made Flesh in their hearts, and the written Word in their hands. These obedient ones receive the precious gift of *'an ear to hear'* what the Spirit is saying, and they *'turn not away back'* faint-heartedly. Isaiah is clear on this *(Is. 50:4,5)*. We have assurance; He will speak with us, and correct us, because we have union with Christ … *but he that is joined unto the Lord is one spirit (1 Cor. 6:17).*

Hearing from the Lord brings with it responsibility, and this is strong meat. Toying with legalism and tradition 'just because the Bible says' could keep us from our true calling. Danger signals should flicker immediately we hear 'Yes, but you must understand, this is by implication …' or 'It goes without saying.' Interpretation and context is a grave consideration, but even more so is the direct word from God, which He by diverse means impart to those who can take the strong meat. God seeks the humble and steadfast as His working tools, but will also speak and work through those He deems fit for a particular purpose and situation as and when it pleases Him, and this is His sovereign prerogative—but work He will. How often the Lord moves through the least likely and the most unexpected!

I now know with clarity of mind that any religious person who considers himself a Christian cannot claim citizenship of the New Jerusalem unless he is of Royal birth. He has no ground to stand on if he cannot bear truthful witness to being reborn, in the full sense of the term *(John 3:1-13)*. If not, in both the spiritual realm and the secular world, he is in fact, a disabled person for he cannot perceive, see (:3), and he cannot enter (:5) the Kingdom of God.

3

THE HOUND OF HEAVEN

Someone Cared Enough

My personal history is of no consequence, but does carry weight in building the case of Sarah and her legacy.

Sometime, somewhere, someone cared enough to be burdened with my lostness—sufficiently so as to carry my pitiful state to the Father. The burden found utterance in prayer and, with Jesus interceding at the right hand of God, there was no way in which the Father's attention could ever be diverted from my lost soul and the decision I alone could make.

I am omitting a lengthy and dramatic case history, yet I must give a short personal account to support the categorical statement that I am representative of thousands upon thousands going through the rituals of Sunday school, catechism, confirmation, church attendance and Holy Communion, of getting married, and bringing babies to the christening font, seeing my children off to Sunday school, of seeing them in their own turn go through the same cycle of church life (including the burial services) without a personal confrontation with Jesus Christ and the inevitable, final, point-of-no-return decision.

Oh Father! Just what does it take to come to grips with fostered inconsistencies, to stop wasting time and opportunities, letting precious souls slip through our fingers? The intensity and passion of Jeremiah lamenting for the lost of Israel can be as deeply expressed by only those who are flooded with the Presence of the Son, and who can discern the real need and identify with the torment of a seeking soul *(Lam.2:18,19)*. Such a rare one had knelt under a wild fig tree alongside a dusty trail in the virgin bush of Northern Rhodesia for my sake—and I never knew this until many, many years later.

No Amount Of Flogging

The degrees of obduracy in people vary. Rooted inhibitions are nothing but *a refuge of lies, a hiding place (Is.28:17,18)*. Understand this: harbouring personal and religious hang-ups is to uphold a covenant with spiritual death and we have much to suffer and learn before yielding to Truth.

The true intercessor is irresistibly drawn to the secret place of the Most High. Such is the burden on him that he feels pressurized, emptied, his person severed from his spirit, his perceptions not his own but those of Another, his whole being flooded with the crucial task at hand. He finds his prayer impregnated by the Holy Spirit. What transpires is beyond human comprehension, a happening coming from within and without, undeniably from the Source of all life. A miracle is wrought only by Divine intervention, for no flesh can do this amazing thing. No amount of flogging or persuasion can make a horse drink water if the need does not well up from within.

How strange that the world judges, and judges correctly! Show the world a fake Christian and they know it. Show the world a genuine Christian copping out, and they know it, for each man is, without exception, his own advertisement. My personal set of rules were neither fake nor genuine, simply, they were mixed and the world read me for what I was—a hypersensitive, self-conscious, pain-in-the-neck with distinct feelings of guilt, remorse, hunger, expectation, wonderment and eagerness. I ascribed the feelings so often surfacing as a natural propensity to the poetic. A dreamer and a visionary? Greek mythology of all things! Smartly fooling myself with fake interest in Keats and Shelley, Wordsworth, I became a miserable quasi-intellectual—*the hiding place always is a flimsy shelter of lies!* Unhappiness, hurt, rebellion, tears, insecurity, rejection, distrust, turmoil!

But the Hound of Heaven was on the hunt. I fled Him another twenty-odd years and finally gave up trying to change myself. It is a great step forward when you can face yourself ruthlessly, painful as it is. Half-measures and half-truths is a serious obstruction in this matter for it works on the same principle as to scapegoat someone else for your failures—so save yourself time and pain and put the blame where it belongs.

Sick at heart, I even stopped trying to love myself for it was fixed in my mind that no one else did, either. I was an open target simply because I knew nothing about demonic assault. Where I come from, the subject does not exist. Erratic and superficial efforts at being a disciplined, exemplary Christian were futile. It did not earn me the esteem my impoverished petty self so desperately craved. It was plain, downright self-indulgence, under the guise of religion, and I was a hungry duck for any sharp shooter luring and selling false doctrine. But I could not still a longing within me. Truth is, I was to learn that one never stops longing and yearning for His presence.

'You are a seeker.' The friendly, chance, innocuous remark hit home, hard and deep, and in an instant, inexplicably, all fell into place: I had fallen in love with a Person. With a mysterious, elusive Person whom *I myself was hunting!* Whose Name had wafted in and out of my conscious thinking over many years of precious time wasted. In addition, I would not even know how to embrace Him should I find Him. How does one do it? You see, where I come from, no one ever said.

I was fortunate. The Lord paid *me* a personal visit and I capitulated; I did not need 'lessons.'

'There is in every man a lesser one, and his presence stinks in the sun.' The cruellest period of my life, surprisingly, then began—the fight with Mrs. I-Me-Mine. And yet I knew I would never be the same again; for me everything had changed

Since August 1971, the Way has become no smoother. I find it growing painfully steeper, yet with an unmistakable pull upward for the Lord irresistibly draws us ever higher and closer.

Take heart, dear one, flying becomes less sporadic and more consistent and satisfying—we *know* we will get *There*, and will stay *There* forever more!

4

CALLING THE BLUFF

Asking WHY

Building the case for 'Sarah's Tent' begins with asking why people think as they do. Why in the world have things turned out as they have? Why do we so readily accept teaching without personal investigation? Why are we not engaged in serious prayer, and why do we find it so difficult to wait on the Lord?

Do we think of revelation as a commodity readily available upon request? The truth is there all the time, but we do not ask for revelation on specific issues of the Word, and so we do not receive. If we do receive, it is all too often more comfortable to remain silent, appease the herd instinct, and bask in congenial surroundings. Are we willing to be corrected? Perhaps we run shy of the possibility of being exposed as a 'phoney' and how we shun the responsibility that accompanies the mantle of prophet! Why? *Because we walk in fear of man and not in fear of God.*

Of course, not every prophet is of God and we should welcome investigations, and invite the Holy Spirit to unmask error. Personal interest is always cloaked in fear of what other people say, but when the Holy Spirit does impart, obedience demands all human trepidation be discarded. Or perhaps, we do not really understand what 'church' is all about, and run eagerly to spout prematurely or inappropriately what we think we have received?

Walking by 'revelation within the heart' changes everything—the person and the walk.

Scorn And Scoffing

Thousands of sincere Christians are not scholars of Greek and Hebrew and have no access to the original texts. They must needs rely on those translations within easy reach and come to their own conclusions, or accept verbatim what they hear from the qualified should these be questioned. We cannot agree with everything coming our way but must be mindful that the Holy Spirit is a free agent and ever ready to touch areas we have overlooked, did not know existed, or never expected Him to sort out.

I am not a women's lib, nor an ultra-feminist, and neither does a spirit of rebellion bother me; I do not have a problem with the Word of God, yet I do expect to spark off scoffing and male resentment, for what you are being shown does not fall into the usual, the agreed and the accepted. Conventional religious practitioners, having made apocryphal analysis and in depth study of the Holy Bible, will be posing questions as to veracity and, yes, my audacity. In fact, at this very moment of writing, my knees are quaking at the prospect of penning what I know must be imparted.

The full history of the Bible leaves one dazed. Suffice it to say, the literary foundations of the Bible have gone through the mill with having hundreds of copyists labouring by hand over centuries and producing what we today have readily available at our fingertips. How many of these translations and versions have been corrupted (however slightly) by human flesh we shall never know—*and this is the vital point when coming to personal conclusions.*

From Scriptures we are taught that God's Word is inviolable. This means God has so protected His written Word that the 'ordinary man in the street' can accept every jot and tittle as from the heart and hand of God alone. Yet Satan, the sly deceiver, knows even a comma can make a difference, and therefore a number of popular versions could become a snare for the unwitting.

Many new translations have in recent years been published as 'another good Bible.' Where words are replaced, the literal meaning expressed in the original manuscript becomes less distinct. Tommy, Fred and Suzie gives preference to easy language and this sells the new bible. Alarmingly, they do not question what they read. If this happens in our day, how much more do we have to consider the possibility of intruding human flesh in previous generations? This has affected every Bible appearing on the scene as much as it affects every believer absorbing the contents of the Book in his hands.

Some ask: what has God revealed to man, how much of His Word has He protected from foolhardy flesh, to what extent has God permitted Satan to attempt drainage and just how many of those involved have been truly used of God?

The answer is: if any discrepancies between God's dealings and man's recording of it have crept in, the fault does not lie with God. He does not work inconsistently and is well able to protect His Truth and impart it as He alone determines. Nevertheless, exegesis rests heavily on man—does he hear himself, the Holy Spirit, or other pervasive influences? We must trust the Lord God and the Holy Spirit, who called worthy synods together and inspired them to assemble us a worthy canon and this, I am telling myself, I must believe.

But added to all of this we have politicians and personal feelings, monasteries and cloisters, cruel rulers and despotism, craftiness and fanatical rivalry, before, medieval, today. Professional vying and jealousy never end with decisive 'for or against' arguments; too many questions have been raised and left without satisfactory, conclusive answers. Theological differences are legion.

Suffice it to say: *in the beginning was the Word, and the Word was with God, and the Word was God Himself (John 1: 1-5).*

What is God saying about all of this? He has given us His Son and His Holy Spirit as our full assurance—His perfect and complete answer to all we may ask or need.

I am returning you to the first paragraph of Chapter 1 and at the same time filling my lungs for the plunge into hot water for as from this point on another unwelcome controversy is being added to Mosaic history—we are going to exhume dear Adam once again and see how his negligence of sweet Eve rock old beliefs.

5

WHEN THE PENNY DROPS

What Does He Do With It

Embedded beliefs based on illusion resist uprooting and therefore uproar from male quarters will not come as a surprise; negative responses to the positive cannot be seen as self-defence but rather as an overflow of deception, of the darkening of the mind.

We are washed clean by the Blood of Jesus, and reconciled with the Father, and still we accept much of the lies of Satan, making them our own and *living them out as 'life in the spirit!'*

The rebellion in the Garden has even further consequences: a satanic agenda lies hidden in ensuing over-ruling male pride and lordship, which has been taken for granted by the male gender and thrust upon females through all ages. It is interesting and wise to observe objectively how these rebellious tentacles stretch into the end-time tent of modern Sarah.

There hardly is a woman who would want her man wishy-washy. Good! And there is hardly a Godly woman who would not want to bask in the security, the leadership and authority of her Godly husband—as God had pre-ordained. Nevertheless, WHAT A MAN DOES WITH HIS NATURAL DOMINANCE AND **HOW HE HANDLES IT** is a matter of grave concern for it directly affects the Bride of Christ.

The Vital Issue Of Submission

Sit back comfortably and enjoy the interaction of a small party of couples, friends together. Now listen for undertones, for remarks or sweet little jokes at the partner's expense. Relaxed and with drinks in hand, the ingrained, casual, assumptive dominance of males, and the simmering rebellion females exude, will unconsciously surface and become evident to the observer.

Feeling threatened, a woman may turn quiet and inward, or openly nasty. Or, to hold her ground, she may project her femininity and resort to provocative sexual subtleties. Many unsaved women draw and hold male attention this way. Proximity plays a formidable role: Eve certainly has effective weapons up her sleeve! This is rather a sad way of obtaining acknowledgement, power or esteem, and does not fall short of manipulation. However, a study of verbal and body language is not restricted to psychiatrists and psychologists, for we are graced with the Holy Spirit who reveals much more.

Bickering serves to stab and wound; and even indulged with a laugh it still remains in poor taste. It expresses bottled up resentment and gives vent to dormant anger. It seldom falls short of the insulting. Awareness of the Indwelling Christ is lost with futile arguments and we may well weep at the things men and women say and do to each other, whether in or out of wedlock, privately or publicly, believers or not.

The Church will have to put all accommodating niceness aside and come down to brass tacks in their teaching: *the vital issue of 'submission' has to be re-addressed, and done so with clear-cut definition.* Therefore, married couples calling on the Ruach Hakodesh to take over and take care of them will have to determine and re-adjust their individual concept of 'submission and obedience.'

Her Desire

Any form of selfish control, under the guise of parental or spousal love, is an ungodly force drawing its operating power from a willing or ignorant victim.

Women are not blameless, and the part Eve plays in daily drama is life or death to those around her. She does not dare foster double standards, nor take a neutral stand to either physical or emotional abuse, for moving into the grey area of apathy produces lifelessness (a direct offspring), and spiritual death follows in its wake.

The intention of this book is not to decry males. A small percentage of the species only are heinous, meaning utterly wicked and odious; these do exist, they do operate, we do have them in our midst, but the same is true of women.

A wrathful God pronounced: *thy desire shall be to thy husband and he shall rule over thee (Gen.3:16).* The illustrious Moses was the first to document what is known as the Book of Genesis and from the very first transmittal of the Adamic happenings, the pronouncement was presented and documented as inviolable Divine decree. Thus it became acceptable, irrefutably a Law, and deemed unalterable Holy Scripture.

Man's concept of ruling, without spiritual purpose, is warped. Woman has been graced with abundance in spheres, realms, and territory to which Man does not have entry. He is not built to accommodate or exercise such extraordinary equipment and without the delicate, exquisite instrumentation as is hers to meet his needs; he is neither kept nor whole. Woman does, in fact, clothe Man. She is a sheaf to him as is a sheaf to a sword: *a woman shall compass a man (Jer.31:22).*

A Disabling Law

Vulgar details are uncalled for—shocking statistics are proof enough. The majority of defenceless women, from the frailest of aged to the smallest babe, have suffered emotional misuse, or the brutal depravity of abusers, including rape. In the face of extensive and irrefutable evidence, even men of sound reasoning will still defend their absoluteness.

The toughest and the more important job have been allotted to woman whom man seeks to rule. (He does!) When it comes to women, many Christian men use the Bible literally as yardstick when in fact he should know better: he takes his first in all, yet in the end she who follows is in fact first. He is protector and provider; she is prop and progenitor. Man! You may feel safe and in command, and the ugly ones may smirk in smugness, but beware lest God remove your self-erected prop! It could turn out to be more than a mere tumble, for if you are married, then, in the eyes of God you are neither whole nor perfect without her

The position of being first does not reduce the value of what follows. It stands to reason that the first in anything can hold no other position until it is replaced by the next. *Adam was first formed, then Eve. And Adam was not deceived but the woman being deceived was in the transgression (1Tim.2:13,14).*

A strong principle operates in the game 'Follow-my-leader' we played as children. The game is typical of how the first leads the second, third, and all are expected to follow the same line of example. The idiom 'First come first served' proves the principle. It is not about being served first because you arrived first. No, it is about being first and therefore being the first to serve the second, third, and all the rest! On principle then, Adam should in the first place have been an example to Eve and serve her a demonstration on obedience. He did not.

Last Adam, our Lord Jesus, is by no means secondary to the first created man. Jesus was *foreordained before the foundation of the world, but was manifest in these last times for you (1 Pet.1:20).* His service is of such divine quality and purpose that He could lay down His life here and so impart His own eternal Life (rebirth and restoration) to those who follow Him, therefore His life is a demonstration of the Father's required standards. First Adam had befuddled his exemplifying mission.

Adam, oh Adam! What *have* you done!

If we profess the Holy Bible, then we must get this one thing straight: *God created from His heart when He made man, and He made woman for man*

But now we must get something else also straight: Adam was the first man God created, but he was only the ***penultimate*** creation. God delighted in creating woman and bringing her to the man. He created her last for a purpose: The creative genius of God kept the best for last because ***ultimately*** from that union He wanted the Earth filled with spiritual progeny in His likeness. In Jesus we are restored to God's desire in Adam—we have eternal life in His likeness, the ultimate purpose of our existence.

Translators, scholars and scribes, expounders and pundits, all at some period in time have done their share of nit picking and hair-splitting in frantic search for the meaning behind the meaning of every jot and tittle. No word, verse or passage have escaped the attention, healthy or otherwise, of those people who have participated on human level in giving us the Bible as we now have it in circulation.

Yet, how is it that one does not hear or read of references made to, or come across any queries concerning a few words omitted by Eve in her discourse with the serpent in the Garden?—Missing words apparently to have escaped the notice of researchers, of those theologians immersed in exegesis, and of those parchment collectors who profess to know ancient mysteries.

Awesome moments, and indelibly imprinted on one's mind when first noted—the tragedy hitting Eve in the Garden has repercussions beyond human assessment. *Genesis 2 and 3* as given in the King James Version, read by millions and believed by as many to be the true Word of God … and now we have to shrug and accept the learned conclusion: 'yes, but you see, she said it by implication'?

Note the difference in contents between the following two passages, because right here we have the crux, the key to the abuse and subjugation of Woman. We will eventually see it falling into place:

And the Lord God commanded the man, saying, Of every tree of the garden thou mayest freely eat: But of the tree of the knowledge of good and evil, thou shalt not eat of it: for in the day that thou eatest thereof thou shalt surely die (Gen.2:l6,17).

And the woman said unto the serpent, we may eat of the fruit of the trees of the garden: But of the fruit of the tree which is in the midst of the garden,

God hath said, Ye shall not eat of it, neither shall ye touch it lest ye die (Gen.3:2,3)

PART TWO

EVE

... and brought her to the man

(Gen.2:22)

1

WHAT PRICE RESPECT?

Statements Of Fact

If the penny drops, and you see this, you will be mocked either openly, or subtly (painfully worse.) It has been said: **'Man has made of himself a law unto woman—a disabling law in the unregenerate state ...**

For of whom a man is overcome, of the same he is brought in bondage (2 Pet.2:19b).(used in another translation: 'worsted' meaning to get the better of, defeat, outdo./Ox.Afr. *verslaan, oorwin, wen, klop, uitstof, onderspit delf.* R.D).

In all history of mankind, Eve has been grossly abused. Her qualities have been ridiculed and aborted. She has largely contributed to this and no attempt is made to exonerate her share of the plight in which she finds herself.

To make a statement of fact: there has never been any meaningful check on male presumption. Subjugation of woman has always been unlicensed and openly perpetrated. Why? Because the agenda is Satanic in origin, a lie fed and kept alive by ignorance of what God originally intended for Man.

The legendary impact of this one woman, this first one, has reverberated down the ages with such assailing repercussions that modern Eve is still staggering under the weight of her shattered image. The Biblical thrust of the encounter with the Evil One in the Garden of Eden does not quell the damage done by folkloric accounts, if not surpassing it in horrendous implications for Eve. Undeniably, documentation has been an efficient and well-oiled conveyor belt for a neatly packaged carton containing both Eve and overwhelming circumstantial evidence—deciding factors for all legalists. It has earned her the contempt of millions.

In the eyes of the world, it has left her not equal in worth, but secondary in consideration, if not much less: disposable, dispersible, and dispensable.

The respect and acknowledgement Eve receives depends entirely on when and where she finds herself: the time in terms of centuries, the world in terms of environment, and civilization in terms of culture.

Whether it is India and she faces incineration together with her deceased husband for the sake of family honour, whether she is the unwelcome firstborn placed out on the ice packs of the North to freeze, or whether she is the defenceless victim of Internet paedophiles. In Africa, she is the hoer of ground, the pack-donkey and incubator.

Without given a choice, she is bartered on the open market as a baby-girl-cum-slave-cum-concubine. Without voice, she is desensitised to parallel the queen ant. She is regarded as serviceable, considered a convenient commodity, exchangeable in family transaction as future bride irrespective of age. In the Middle Ages she had, to protect her femininity and her person against rape, of dire necessity been forced to wear an iron chastity belt locked to her frame.

Her very person is the brothel—held either forcibly for male pleasure and perversity, or she solicits solely (and stolidly) for the sake of bread and butter. The oldest profession in the world rewards her with nothing but degradation and sickness of heart, only to be cast aside in old age as some rotten, stinking, untouchable article.

In the Americas as recently as the mid 19th century unwedded females of 'lower' class were stripped to the waist, tied to a post and publicly whipped. The reason? She had the misfortune of conceiving when molested. 'Her body' had sinned against a man. There was small hope of retrieve, no pardon, and no mercy if he happened to be her owner and master. She was the slave and as such, public lashing would offset his share of the game—or guilt.

Defenceless as young girl taken captive even in our times, Eve is subject to atrocities Almighty God only can avenge. How many searching days and sleepless nights have filled and changed the lives of anxious parents, and what was their contribution?

A worldwide phenomenon through all ages: she is held under duress in harems, a toy to the whims and passions of those who hold her for life. Abducted, sold. Lost.

South African statistics show one rape every 30 seconds. The figure can be higher for not every woman wants to disclose her humiliation and shame.

According to Mary Wollstonecraft Godwin (1759–1797)[1] females in her times were not permitted a university education. Women were not permitted to

---

1.   The Vindication of the Rights of Women

enter the medical profession. Law forbid married females the possession of property. Legally, women were not entitled to a divorce, not even on the grounds of her husband committing adultery. According to law a husband had full claim on the salary his wife earned; she had no option but hand it over on demand. If a married woman separated from her spouse, she had no legal rights whatsoever in claiming her children. If the male spouse left his wife, he was under no legal obligation to support her financially.

Omnipotent God deemed it fit to make His Son manifest through the physical body of an ordinary woman so He could walk as Deity in our world—a Man amongst men, and Satan retaliates in fury by insulting the incarnation of Christ. He invokes a spirit of lust in man to rape the body and mind of woman.

Ad Infinitum

If ever the Bible has given us a disgusting account of inhuman treatment and callous disregard, then we find it in *Judges 19* with emphasis on *verses 24 and 25*. (Please to compare with other translations)*:*

Behold, here are my daughter a maiden, and his concubine; them I will bring out now and humble ye them and do with them what seemeth good unto you, but with this man do not so vile a thing.

But the men would not hearken to him; so the man took his concubine, and brought her forth unto them; and they knew her and abused her all the night until the morning and when the day began to spring they let her go

She was abused, mauled, died, and then shredded. She was a woman. Considered disposable, dispersible and dispensable.

Only in recent years have human rights taken on shape and size, receiving wide and enthusiastic public attention. But the devil is cleverly and dangerously tipping the scale to the other extreme—unless the Church recognizes the strategy betimes. Satan is now pushing the female sex into independence and contempt for authority. This, in essence, is Adam in rebellion and a denial of the authority of God.

2

THE BELIEVING EVE

Single Women

Nothing about Eve's person is recorded. We assume she was beautiful, because God looked at her and admired His creation; she was perfect. We know nothing about her personal feelings and emotions, but we do know she had an inquiring mind.

It is held by some, and most unfairly, that sex was the apple Eve held out to Adam. Not true. Be ye corrected: *And God blessed them, and God said unto them, Be fruitful, and multiply, and replenish the earth (Gen.l:28).*

There always are, and always will be, a good number of single women in every congregation or fellowship. They usually are in the majority and can generally be described as fringe-seekers simply because they so faithfully, passively, perhaps erratically, often enthusiastically, drift along with every turn and decision, always ready to take their tea-turns, do their stint at pancakes and bun parties.

Many of these suffer loneliness and find sustenance and security in small vying cliques; available and ready to do the good works no one else will undertake They are the busy bees at fund raising efforts and their place in worship and service to the church and community is not to be underrated or despised.

Spiritually Single Women

Then there are the rare few; a small percentage—the seriously committed ones. They are spiritually advanced, speak little, reserve their good reason, know much—and, married to an un-regenerate man. They are not to be adjudged spiritually as a married couple, but being unequally yoked, the reborn woman is as a person single in Spirit.

Does the credibility of these 'spiritually single' women depend on what the leadership understand as 'suitable covering' (referring to the husband)? Is the leadership perhaps underestimating the spiritual level of saintly women who do not involve themselves with extraneous activities in the congregation? And if her husband has an unconvincing walk as 'believer', are they gauging the believing Eve accordingly? If so, then the work of the Holy Spirit is dissipated; the Body is deprived of ministry, and the growth in Spirit of the Church retarded.

Leadership can be so busy maintaining 'God's order, and covering, and submission' that they neglect the Shulamite (the serious ones who seek the presence of the beloved Bridegroom with urgency). *Songs 5:7* describe the ill-judged diligence of these leaders: *The watchmen that went about the city found me; they smote me, they wounded me; the keepers of the walls took away my veil from me*

Zealous and indiscreet, these keepers and watchmen of 'the church' sometimes defeat their object by going too far. A veil and mantle depict intimate and responsible association with the Lord, and it may never, never be violated by religiosity—which always is the fruit of legalism and spiritual pride. In direct contrast to the keepers of the walls we have Hegai, keeper of the women, who prepared, nurtured and cherished the King's future Queen Esther *(Est.2:9,15)*.

The Lord has regard for those women who stand alone in Christ and suffer for it—persecution in the privacy of their homes, socially, and in the congregation where sanctimonious believers sanction harassment under the guise of 'correction' and think of it as good advice, dear.

If it is rebirth standing between partners, she will get no solace or protection from her unregenerate husband in matters spiritual. If the male spouse inflicts emotional abuse then his ire will be further provoked if her walk does not waver. She has only one option: to enter the Rest of God, thereby letting Him complete His perfect works.

Leadership is charged to think well. Sensitive support and consideration are not given to married women who have come to know the Lord in a deep and intimate way and who do not have the privilege of being led into a yet deeper commitment by their husbands *for all men have not faith (2 Thess.3:2). (Romans 9* teaches that God *hardens, makes stubborn and unyielding the heart of—whoever He wills, so His mercy and saving grace can be made known at the right time).*

Nevertheless, difficult and awkward situations develop when one partner remains unresponsive to the call of Christ and far more grievous if the loved one is the head of the house and glued to a pew-warming system, with a tight grip on his key position, and holding all the trump cards in the other hand. Such men find the doctrine of repentance; restitution and total surrender too taxing and resort to religious traditions as a convenient, comfortable and safe haven. **He is bound**. N*o man can enter into a strong man's house and spoil his goods except he will* *first bind the strong man; and then he will spoil his house (Mark 3:27).* Satan will have himself a family … every time a husband and father ignore or twists a God-given truth, Evil zones his wife and zaps his children.

Abuse

Where a husband inflicts both emotional and physical abuse, it may be helpful for the regenerate wife to remember that her partner is a **victim** in the clutches of an evil, merciless and perverse spirit. Separate the person from his deeds—even if it's difficult to see him as God sees him! God loves him as much as He loves all His other suffering ones. Beloved saint, you cannot change your spouse. No one can. Reprogram your mind about saving your husband. Love him with God's agape love and leave him be—difficult, difficult!—but one can tell Father it's okay if nothing spiritual is happening for him. This sets him free and releases both of you for in making this decision you are giving consent to the Holy Spirit to hunt him down without interference. It does not mean you must accept gross misdeeds and nonsense though, but rather to step aside, mentally and spiritually.

I am haunted by the memory of a friend who had no idea, no inkling of the emotional distress his un-awareness caused his family. John was thoughtless. His wife, a re-born woman, stated: 'You won't detect the trait soon, you can't put your finger to the thing, it is so subtle that you have to live with it, experience it, before you see it for what it is. He is driving me up the walls and I can't talk to John, he won't let me. He gets angry. He is always telling me I am only finding fault. He doesn't seem to think or see how this affects all of us. Can it really be that he doesn't know what he's doing? It's like as if he is living in an impenetrable bubble, except of course when he feels he is 'again being insulted'. Then he is quick to jump out of his haze.'

I let Marie talk on. Having known this couple for years and having observed matters building up to the point of no return, I could add to her version but refrained. She would not consider divorce as a solution. Some would say that Marie's problem as his wife, and being re-born, was her inability to cultivate the commendable Christian fortitude—just to give and give of her self—and not to expect anything back in return. This, I know, would be too much to ask of her particular temperament. Besides, I would not recommend anyone *even trying* this futile course of action.

I knew John as a nice person, thoroughly nice and pleasant. This man's feet were planted squarely on firm ground. He did not tolerate abstract topics, call it religion if you want, and scoffed openly at 'overdoing Christians'. No drinking, no smoking. He was a gifted sportsman, competitive by nature, very sociable, successful in his profession and happily engrossed in his hobbies, a good though overly frugal provider, and? And, but.

And John lacked nothing but the ability to place himself with sensitivity in the other man's shoes. He could only see everyone and everything through his own thick lenses, and went whistling on his way in thoughtless un-awareness of ever having stoked the fire and not stirring the stew to keep it from boiling over

I was in a next-door position to watch the drama enfold and am convinced that John could not see, and even if he did, much less examine his role in the vicious circle of their incompatibility. He refused participation in marriage counselling. He flatly rejected professional help and experience teaches that this is a sure indication of trauma deeply embedded in denial because it is too painful to let the truth be dug up and scrutinised. So it just doesn't exist, see?—but eventually this monstrous illusion inexorably takes its toll—and John's frustration with everything and everyone grew.

I still think he never saw himself as the one with the problem and would deny even the possibility thereof. With time I observed how quick John was to take offence and jump to hasty conclusions, convinced he was the one being slighted or insulted. With habitual unawareness having robbed him of fine-tuned discernment, John would then be unrelenting and merciless in defence of himself.

Marie continually implored the Lord to change her. She desperately wanted to be a good wife, and with time developed the unfortunate trait of being too apologetic about everything. She was continually asking John's (and everyone else's) forgiveness; this carried no weight with John and she was losing his respect and her creditability. Tears behind the bathroom door did not help—Marie was also fast losing whatever self-worth she had left.

John, shaking his head, once remarked within hearing: '*Marie gives me all the hell of my life! I just can't understand why she is the way she is, and why she reacts as she does.*' To me John appeared not to sense the discomfit his wife endured, and it seemed never to have struck his mind that Marie had emotional needs of her own. John was genuinely perplexed. He sidestepped engaging with Marie in honest and mutual probing of their individual hang-ups. Unpleasant episodes remained unresolved—for John clearly felt threatened at the prospect of having to look inside himself. His defence mechanism when cornered or confronted was an intimidating blast of quick anger together with the customary accusation flung at his wife that all she could do was find fault. It was a strategy that never failed to work for then Marie, resentful and bitter, immediately retracted behind the bathroom door and the blameless victor would serenely go on his whistling way as if nothing had happened.

Marie had no defence system or mechanism that worked for her. She was easily intimidated and bristled with indignation at what she considered to be injustice and emotional assault. She lashed herself continuously with self-accusation and remorse. Marie sincerely desired to grow spiritually and in this felt she had failed and had made 'many religious mistakes'. She also felt she had failed miserably as mother and as wife. This was not what John wanted, nor what he needed, did I explain. I told her she was hanging on to illusions and giving worth to false demonic presentations, and she was not even near being a 'good Christian' for she was neither doing John any good, nor herself.

I do not know if John ever broke through into discovering his real self, but Marie was open to correction and the Master's incomparable teaching. I have subsequently heard that she is free and soaring, gaining in insight and growing in uncovered skills. Good for her.

Please believe me, I am not pointing fingers and calling from my ivory tower: "Hey you guys! I've arrived! I can see you from where I'm sitting. So watch out! Don't this and don't that!" But I do hold that every human being has a deep pivotal core of secret need, and he/she needs to know what that need is and must permit it to surface and be examined.

The case of thoughtless John endorses my sincere empathy *(deernis)* for men who **needlessly** suffer the whole spectrum of desperation: pain, rejection, contempt, disappointment, frustration, failure, defeat, financial and professional worries, hatred, the whole works and more, and in ignorance of their true need seek release in committing atrocities or indulging unacceptable social practices

These men are trapped not only in the sad condition of their mental state but as a consequence also in the unfortunate circumstances created by that ill-health. The chronic condition of denial, their acute bewilderment, and unidentified misery must be hell on earth.

I am learning about ivory towers ...

Thought-Life

Physically and emotionally abused women are brainwashed, overpowered and controlled by dark forces, their thoughts mill in circles. Are you one of these? You could be of any age—gripped and trapped in a destructive situation because you appear to have no solution? Perhaps no other means of supporting yourself and your children and you cannot think beyond this? Reconsider all options—mistakes will no doubt be made, but wise decisions sprout from correct thinking. This is hardly possible when the mind is frayed and the heart bleeding, yet one's thinking processes *must* first and foremost be addressed.

The mind needs to be re-educated and this is a work done entirely by the Holy Spirit, together with a willingness to be changed. This does not happen overnight and seldom in the way we think it should.

But *don't* load your partner's rubbish on board your own wagon. *Don't* make excuses for him. Don't feel bound to correct his mistakes, or hasten to clear his part of the mess. He alone is responsible for his choices, decisions, and actions. **Getting out of God's way means taking hands off!** You are not the one to rescue him—rather go tip everything at the foot of the Cross, stand aside, and press on to personal restoration.

Come apart

Constructive self-examination takes honesty and determination. Come apart for this examination; take your time and make notes. More notes will follow over time as you press on. Tell Father you are prepared to bring a practical offering, you will not fold spiritual hands in apathy and expect Him to move mightily into your situation, but that you will take active part in His 'reconstruction works'. We receive not because we ask not; also, we often pray amiss. Prayer is the highest priority, so ask for, and expect Divine revelation. The inner man will receive the full truth concerning your situation and afford you discernment. Define and objectively analyse the part you have played in the overall disaster. Repent—and forsake, for if we expect God to move in then we must obey His rules. The power of the Indwelling Christ will surge up to rescue and lead into personal victory when the old man becomes hot, desperate, impulsive, alive and kicking. You will be tempted to react as you have always done before, but the notes you make each day should help to keep you on track

Breaking links

Take courage and carefully consider the next steps forward in your private battle. Closely scrutinize your habits, reactions, prejudices and feelings. Spread it out before the Lord. Look for a pattern in the happenings in your life and your marriage. Do not isolate or concentrate on only one particular instance; there have been repeat performances. Dig into the lessons learnt, separate real guilt from false accusation, and do not foster negative introspection. Time and again you have found yourself walking into the same trap; hooked into the same inter-action. Well then, break the pattern of your habitual responses with a very differ-ent one. Call this a strategic counter-attack, if you like, but break a few links of the chain and be prepared for surprising results.

Ask yourself if you are not perhaps feeding demonic activities at the cost of your spiritual strength and dignity. It could be that you have not yet acknowl-edged the truth to yourself: 'I am a reborn child of God, washed and protected by the Blood of Jesus and therefore I am NOT a victim but a soldier in full battle armour for the King. His values are mine and I do NOT accept what is happen-ing. I do NOT have to comply with what is being perpetrated. There is a way out and my Father is the only One who can, and will, take me out.'

Years of mistakes and painful episodes, of experience, of growth and acquired wisdom filtering through from Above *(Jam.1:5)*, all are poured into the moment of now. Here, and now, influence and shape the next half hour, tomorrow, next year. The initial steps in warfare you take now will bring you to the next steps. Satan will also use others to undermine or deter your determined walk, so do not find it strange when the more you move toward the truth about yourself, the more will offence and resentment trigger off in dissolute people. Resentment is an insidious type of jealously; remember, and this is important: you do not have to explain or defend your case to others.

The answer to every threatening situation lies within the individual, and no outsider should be encouraged to plan or stimulate offensive tactics. The ten-dency is to talk to anyone who is prepared to listen, and 'oh shame, dear' our mis-ery. Stop this. And refrain from impulsive talking, for one more surface counsellor added to many other voices confuses sound advice, and in the babble wise counsel will be snatched from you. The Lord has provided experienced and skilled saints in the Body to minister in the particular field of physical and emo-tional abuse, and they will come to your assistance on request.

11 Cor.10:3-5

Spend prime time on these well-known verses: *For though we walk in the flesh, we do not war after the flesh:*

(For the weapons of our warfare are not carnal, but mighty through God to the pulling down of strongholds);

Casting down imaginations, and every high thing that exalts itself against the knowledge of God, and bringing into captivity every thought to the obedience of Christ.

Our fight is against satanic power, a force exercising its influence and aiming at conquest of our whole being. Evil can, and often does, work through another person (who might even be a misled Christian!). You are not fighting flesh and blood. You can only fight when you know who and what you are fighting, and the strategy it employs. The devil adroitly and repeatedly uses the same ploy for the same person. If it has worked before, then he banks on having it work again. Satan only changes the way he looks; he stays small and mean and few see him coming betimes. He is recognized only after his minions have befouled everything and gleefully left the scene—until next time, if you let him.

Ask God to reveal to you those strongholds you may have overlooked and start pulling them down. It means you must face every painful truth and neither refute nor side step. Sustained warfare is required. An eye-opener may leave you disillusioned and weak, but this is where God is strong and moves in—often the last hours are the worst before His answer manifests.

Ask Father to apply His two-edged sword and sever your spirit from all soul-ties. Your spiritual director will advise and assist you in this.

Absolute personal honesty will pay tremendous dividends when you consider the next questions. If you are ruthlessly determined to get to the root causes of your problems, then you will consider the implications very seriously

A. **Are you playing the martyr?** Yes? Then stop the act immediately.

B. **Do you indulge in super-spirituality?** Define between non-retaliation and non-acceptance of intimidation. Be careful now, or a spirit of religion will have you accepting control or abuse for the wrong reasons!

C. **Are you not perhaps one of those who are getting exactly what you desire?** Make sure you agree with your answer, because if you identify a dependency on inflicted abuse to satisfy an inner need for such treatment, then you are in deep trouble. Don't side step this issue; there is great work to be done.

So then, get to know about the Jezebel-Ahab syndrome and fight it, or it will rule you all your life. For a long time you will need staunch and involved support in this battle. A fascinating account of control and manipulation is found in *1 Kings 16:29 onward, and followed in 11 Kings 9:33 etc*

In short: Ahab thrives on Jezebel. Ahab is a spirit seeking to be ruled, or used, by a stronger personality. Jezebel is a controlling spirit, always taking over and asserting itself—could be that the individual through whom Jezebel operates is not consciously aware of the condition. Jezebel needs to gain its own (selfish) ends and it sucks on to the passive, ingratiating spirit of a resentful yet complying Ahab, who will not or cannot, take responsibility for him/her self. More often than not, the interaction is extremely subtle and Ahab's quaking battle for freedom (having been made aware of the reality of the bondage) is heartrending. For the weakened spirit of Ahab to extricate him or her, to take firm stand, and face Jezebel (or any other form of illegal control), remains a painful and terrifying venture.

Should you recognize Ahab at work in your personal experience, then start pulling the stronghold down. The key to freedom is righteousness. Begin by setting firm and healthy boundaries for yourself. Your "No!" must be appropriate and decisive. **Then stick to it.** Make no excuses for your decisions in any matter. The inclination to be apologetic about everything should also be denied. Do not permit feelings of guilt for the choices other people make in response to your boundaries. Never hold yourself responsible for another person's reactions choices and reactions.

The Jezebel-Ahab interaction takes on different colours in different settings. On the one hand, Jezebel will surface and reveal itself when contradicted, opposed or thwarted, and will most likely then employ the effective tactics of soul-force (even resort to physical or verbal abuse) to overrule and run your boundaries down. Sulks, tears, cold-shouldering or withdrawal are common clues indicating Jezebel in action. The Afrikaans term '*stil-stuipe*' is an amazingly apt description. This ploy is manipulative, very successful, and intended to make Ahab feel so guilty that she (or he) would rather dance to Jezebel's tune than suffer rejection or being ignored. Dependent Ahab will even fawn to regain favour, playing right into the hand of Jezebel, and so the vicious circle repeats itself.

On the other hand, Jezebel will, when opposed, or exposed, react with seething resentment and animosity. Boiling anger will build up to the red-hot act of cutting itself loose from Ahab, totally and irrevocably. It then seeks fresh fields and a new Ahab to conquer and control.

However, the behavioural pattern of the Ahab spirit rebounds: its victim suffers an agony of self-accusation and self-condemnation, leaving him/her immersed in self-pity, guilt, helplessness and inadequacy, willing to pay *anything* to restore the Jezebel-Ahab relationship. Stop right here! **Refusal to return to bondage** is the greatest test in the battle for freedom.

Zech.8:16 carries a strong injunction: *these are the things that ye shall do: speak ye every man the truth to his neighbour, execute the judgment of truth and peace in your gates.* **Speak only the truth to Jezebel and confront Ahab at the same time.** Thus, with Ahab also exposed and the real you slipping from its clutching influence over your personality and life, any partnership operating on this demonic level will be brought into startling perspective and, not surprisingly, with far reaching repercussions for all parties involved. Not pleasant—but with the Lord in charge, always rewarding.

You could be either Jezebel or Ahab, and to face up to the condition is the only possible route of escape. But we have the Name of Jesus! *And his name through faith in his name hath made this man strong, whom ye see and know; yea, the faith which is by him hath given him this perfect soundness in the presence of you all (Acts.3:16).*

However, we are out of the will of God if/when we dishonour the place and position of our spouse. Each pit of humiliation suffered is schooling of the spirit, and confidence in the flesh must be pushed aside. This makes waiting on God difficult, more so when He has withdrawn and we cannot hear Him. The separation is felt—as if one's spirit is 'unseen' and in a place unknown to others but, WAIT—and let the God Who possesses life speak. God will judge us in the secret place, and no man shall know it. He is great!

Ps.91:1

He that dwelleth in the secret place of the most High shall abide under the shadow of the Almighty.

The following passage, precious, was picked up somewhere along the Way, author unknown: 'ABIDE: the word has great depth—: to endure without yielding. The simplistic root means WAIT AND ENDURE: continue, dwell, remain, be present, stand, tarry, to stay in a given state. The nature of the vine is transmitted through the branch by virtue of a 'process of abiding' or **remaining connected**—the fruit will bear the characteristics of the central stock—to remain vitally and intimately connected to Jesus Christ: a real and vital relationship and utter abandonment to Him, and **in an unbroken state'.**

Ask to see from God's perspective; because seeing from man's perspective induces even more mistakes. This is harsh on the old man. If we are determined to go on with the Lord, then this painful process of learning to walk the Way will never end; the only consolation and reward is a tear-filled journey of joy and growth *unto the measure of the stature of the fullness of Christ (Eph.4:13).*

Every infant falls as it learns to walk, and sprinters trip and fall as easily. When least expected, of course. Those running a marathon never attempt the exacting race impulsively; they are disciplined, well exercised and circumspect, they are mindful that premature boastings could bear unexpected pitfalls. The just shall live by faith. *Therefore let him that thinketh he standeth take heed lest he fall.(1 Cor.10:12).*

It is expedient that mature and experienced sisters in Christ should become involved in praying the spiritually single married woman through the inevitable trials and crises. One could describe this woman as a spiritual widow and *Jam.1:27* encourage us to visit, help and care for the widows in their afflictions and needs.

This then is the body in full function: where a member is wounded and bleeding, the rest of the body is also affected in some way or another and logical steps are to be taken toward total recovery, for the insidious work of the Evil One permeates the whole body if given a chance.

The Real Dilemma

Fortunate indeed is the godly man who is enjoying a wholesome and rewarding relationship with his most special person—the woman he loves, his wife.

Being of a singular and special brand himself, he will readily make time to ponder on those who are not as fortunate. A man of rare insight may not find it so difficult to identify with the embarrassment, the covering-up, and the extra layers of make-up, of a troubled woman. If this man has moved beyond subjugation on the grounds of gender as the norm expects of him, he will place himself with sensitivity in the shoes of one who is constantly subdued and will know in his spirit that all is not good that looks good. 'They are every week in church, are they not? Could it be …?'

He will understand the slow strangling and eventual death of initiative and enterprise, the crumbling of robust self-confidence. He will hear the whispered hammering: be submissive to your husband in all … in all … in all … she has to listen to me … to me … to me …

The devil is not particular whom he uses, or in what way he messes people up. His aim is to keep believers in his power, even if only partially. Just keep them a bit handicapped, and soul-force is as effective a means as anything else. Ignorance and deception does the rest.

Soul-ties and soul-force are rarely recognized for what they are, and as seldom understood. Soul-tie is an incredibly powerful stream of influence running between two psyches, and draws its energy from a feeling of one-ness and likeness. Any deep experience shared form a bond and sexual intercourse easily ranks highest on the list. Sexual union generates a driving energy, and with certain people could develop into a love-hate tie. This type of mutual control between two persons can be compared with the suffocating coils of a boa.

When married couples are not of the same level, or ilk, then the plot thickens dramatically. Satan sits ready and waiting for the kill, and he never gives up: the faith and steadfast plod forward of the spiritual spouse will be attacked for the aim always is to destroy faith, and soul-tie will usurp the believer's fear of God if left unchecked.

The fear of breaking loose from soul-force and soul-tie is incapacitating. If the subjugated partner is a woman, more so if she has small children, then her fears will smother logic and sustained resistance in spiritual warfare. Her commitment to Jesus may be sacrificed to appease this other cankerous force and here is the real problem. The intensity of her emotional suffering is tempered by her degree of self-composure and self-discipline but always, always is she aware of a sense of divided loyalties.

For what knows thou, o wife, whether thou shalt save thy husband? (l Cor.7:16).

Whether it be right in the sight of God to hearken unto you more than unto God, judge ye (Acts.4:19)

For they that are after the flesh do mind the things of the flesh; but they that are after the Spirit the things of the Spirit.

For to be carnally minded is death; but to be spiritually minded is life and peace.

Because the carnal mind is enmity against God for it is not subject to the law of God, neither can it be.

So then they that are in the flesh cannot please God.

But ye are not in the flesh, but in the Spirit if so be that the Spirit of God dwell in you. Now if any man have not the Spirit of God, he is none of his (Rom.8:5-9).

If she is reborn, her whole being yearns and hungers for more of full obedience to the indwelling Presence. Her husband does not share this longing for total commitment to Jesus. The enlightenment welling up from within her finds instant and spontaneous connection with the written Word and she is being taught of the Holy Spirit, but the world does not share her vision, her joy, her delight, and it is heart-rending when the one all-important person in her life, her husband, does not either—for he cannot appreciate her vision and her new life.

Now she finds herself on an emotional seesaw and facing her at the other end is Self-accusation and Guilt.

Tradition has taught her she is not to oppose her husband, and religiosity tells her to submit to her husband in all, and the overwhelming majority of Christians propagate this view. Therefore, in her church, the Eve who ties herself with ropes to the altar *(Ps. 118:27)*, might well be misunderstood, for fellow believers may not yet have ripened to an understanding of 'submission.'

It is interesting to know that the altar in the Old Testament speaks of the Cross in the New Testament, and in tying one's self to the altar, one will inevitably experience the cut of the sword. Severance is rarely pleasant because it is a cutting off of *everything,* and this is a pre-requisite for following the Cross.

The Light permeating her being will not be denied, and the seesaw leaves our little woman dangling in mid-air. Conflict continues to accuse her of disloyalty to her husband; that she is working at variance, has another goal, pulling in another direction, marching to a different drumbeat, and False Guilt hammers her conscience with That Thing Called Submission.

This is the point where Eve either grows or cracks.

If she succumbs to False Guilt, then Control steps in through the opening and the stronger, unregenerate husband begins to tie his strings tighter because the presence of the Indwelling Christ in his home threatens his zone of spiritual comfort (in which all unregenerate swaddle.)

If 'poor, poor Eve' retains some spark, the couple will tirelessly grate and manipulate each other, straining and pecking to hold top position. The seasoned spiritual partner, however, should soon wizen up to evil tactics and smartly put an end to demonic activities, for when he/she has grown to understand why the Lord says *'come out from amongst them'* a bickering climate will no longer be tolerated or fed.

Spiritual Eve will discern and not slavishly succumb to carnal submission, and beloved carnal Adam is bound to object. Yet, if she is reborn and exposed for a prolonged period to the double standards her carnal Christian husband habitually maintains in their home, she may begin to doubt the soundness of her faith. The male, having the more dominant characteristics, instinctively takes the lead in everything, but oh! beware your soul, dear Adam, lest *you* are the one who has married a Jezebel!

3

WARM FUZZIES AND COLD PRICKLIES

Ignorance Or Intent

Paul makes a personal contribution in some of his letters, and rightly so. This, however, has on occasion brought the seventh chapter of his first Epistle to the Corinthians under fire. It is possible for a married couple to come to terms and make mutual decisions according to what the Holy Spirit is saying to the regenerate spouse who, obviously, will have a high regard for marriage as instituted by God, but respect for matrimony will also have the regenerate spouse considering the consequences of divorce in depth. Verse 15b of this chapter suggests the possibility of Paul's personal view, whereas Matthew records Jesus as stating clearly that the only grounds for divorce is adultery.

However, if this good, dear, beloved husband is firmly entrenched in the only armchair and at the same time also fully convinced of his standpoint being flawless, especially concerning his religion, then he will not shift his ground; and inevitable then the suppression or dissipation of the work of the Holy Spirit in their relationship.

The enemy, if the wife is continually being overruled by the husband, whether he is reborn or not, will not be slow in evoking doubts about her stand in Christ, and one can begin to understand the perplexity of the one suffering emotional abuse inflicted under the guise of religion; at times so sweetly done. This Adam is either blissfully ignorant of his ignorance, or, he wields his dominance with intent, wreaking havoc in the lives of those closest to him. Emotional damage in his family is bound to occur and will inevitably surface, even after a lapse of many years.

Some respected and revered men claim their rights as head and leader and distort the beautiful gift of submission even further. The wives of these men have neither insight nor concept of the evil forces at work, blunting their perception and twisting their willingness to submit into abject emotional captivity, leaving the victim dry of discernment and practical application of wise decision-making.

Can anyone, in any way, convey to another the Presence and the heartbeat of Jesus? The privilege is personal and singular and no other can gauge the quality of the experience. The unregenerate husband is nonplussed, he is perplexed, he notes changes in his partner. He does not understand the depth, or the reality of the supernatural. He now hears the Name of Jesus spoken with reverence and he tires of having his wife engrossed in a subject for whom he has no appetite or aptitude. Her enthusiasm for matters Holy leaves him stone cold.

In fact, their inter-personal reactions had for years run on the same circular track … you do this, and then I say this … I do that and then I can be sure you will.

Now the track has changed considerably. 'you don't want to go with me like you used to … and I can't see why you think it's wrong to …' Bitterness creeps in; resentment, his comfort and his conveniences may have been disturbed, however slightly. He feels he has lost his customary prominence. He feels rejected. Understandable, understandable! He may even conclude she does not love him anymore, at least, not as much as before. Wrong, wrong! She might love him *more than ever before!*

Rebirth of one spouse now has each of the couple walking with a foot in two worlds.

Jesus does this to us.

Without Boundaries

There is a crucial difference between a religion of cultural convenience (traditional) and a God Who is holy, calling us to walk a Way, calling us to a commitment unto death. We are to come out of the snugness and ease of mind that, (being ensconced in the folds of the flock dwelling within the city walls) has been nurtured within us since early childhood. Jesus was crucified outside the city walls. Carnal Adam cannot understand, much less carry, this cross together with his Spirit-filled wife.

But the natural man receiveth not the things of the Spirit of God: for they are foolishness unto him: neither can he know them, because they are spiritually discerned (1 Cor.2:14).

What on earth is a woman to do?

Look around—see the complex nature of man. Really SEE the male of the species, see how tender he can be, how abrupt. Sharing, and so insensitive. Considerate, and at the same time so selfish. He is gentle and so often cold, brutal, loving, assertive and domineering, seldom really interested in his wife and her affairs—yet how he loves her, in his own way!

Satan does not want people to understand the completeness of the redemptive work of Jesus at Calvary. He hates woman the more because she carried the Seed finalising his doom, which we will later discuss. Because Satan is an imitator of everything God does through His Son, he uses the written Word to bring forth a falseness appearing to be the truth but destroys

In a few cases, steeped male reasoning holds that women must accept physical abuse (concomitant with emotional and verbal abuse) as natural to her subordinate position in life. This tendency is a matter of normal conduct with some ethnical groups.

The word subordinate meaning: of inferior importance, of minor importance, underling, under another's control, subservience. This word appears in a few translations, viz. The Amplified Bible *(1 Cor.14:34)*. Note: the N.I.V. Hebrew-Greek Key Study Bible does not use the word 'subordinate.' But for unreasonable Christian men this particular word is incentive, and for their womenfolk, this word employed in a Bible is ominous, lethal. Damage! The common use of the prefix sub-is generally misunderstood, and will be examined later.

The spirit of religiosity wraps itself in a mantle of 'good' and makes it the more effective. 'Sound' male authority is thus well concealed in the teaching of 'God's order', 'covering' and 'submission'—teaching that have over years been stretched to strange limits. False religion is birthed when erroneous teaching and fleshly application of wifely submission is condoned. Hideous if a man practices it. Calamitous if a woman prides herself in it, and spiritually crippled children are inevitable.

Yes, of course .men suffer as much at the hand of women and we shall come to this. But it is beyond any self-reliant, rational, healthy, self-sufficient man ever to fully know the hurt and wounding when a ravaged woman turns to fellow-Christians for warmth and tenderness and is tritely educated from a distant platform: *'Wives, be submissive to your husbands in all!'*

Is this not the panacea, the palliation for every questionable marital situation and every ailing church? Is it not significant that hardly any speaker ever gives an acceptable explanation of what submission really entails? Where to start and where to stop when submitting? To whom does the principle apply and to whom not? Do any attempt to define the boundaries of submission? There are none. But the principle of spiritual submission applies to every man and every woman and the gates of hell cannot prevail against it. It unleashes all the power of God Almighty!

Submission in the spiritual realm means: HAVING THE MIND OF CHRIST.

How we have distorted the meaning of the word 'submission!' How vastly misunderstood, misrepresented and misapplied! This God-given precept has to do with eternal Kingdom values, and not at all with secular standards, personal inconvenience, or loss of face! Jesus submitted to the Father. As a consequence, He walked as ordinary person among ordinary people; He walked as King among kings, in such respect, such awesome holy acknowledgement of His Father that He never claimed any rights for Himself. He never regarded submission as demeaning! It never made of Him a spineless weakling! (1 Cor.2:15,16; Phil.2:5-8; 1 Pet.4:1,2).

4

THE STAGE IS SET

Adding Final Touches

In setting the stage for the Garden of Eden, we must needs add final touches to the décor, for the play is fast building up to the last scene of the saga of all sagas.

About Adam and Eve? Yes—certainly the most well known and most debated of all passages in the Bible up to the advent of Christ.

God said: let us make man in our image, after our likeness and let them have dominion … in the image of God created he him; male and female created he them.(Gen.1:26,27).

God commanded the man not to eat of the tree of knowledge of good and evil. Not a request this, but a command that leaves no room for anything else but obedience—*or thou shalt surely die*—unequivocally *(Gen.2.18).*

God is pleased with the man He made. He decides this man Adam needs a woman in his life. Yes, Adam is perfectly made, but with an equally perfect match to meet him with help, Adam would be perfectly perfect. The Amplified Bible describes the helper-meet as SUITABLE, ADAPTED, COMPLETING.

Don't smile, gentlemen! The crucial point we may not miss here is that we are looking at the spiritual qualities required of the Bride of the Lamb of God and if we want to be part of this Bride, then we must get serious. Therefore, get rid of every man-made structure that buddies up with comfort and a religion of convenience. This injunction includes the tag declaring 'MEN ONLY' in any areas of thinking, and any systems of clubs. There is a time and place for everything, but never may our approach to life exclude our spouse.

If any of the secularly built pyramids and systems are so superbly efficacious in soothing a man's self-image and he deems it necessary to join an Adult Boy's Club, then he has the type of mentality that reduces his help-meet to the status of a functional appliance. For sure, it is good, healthy and vitalizing to be with other sound, wholesome men, but not when hankerings swap wife and home in any degree for guys and fun—in which case the male spouse is telling the wide world he is immature and irresponsible. Individuals advertise themselves, but unfortunately our labels are pinned on our backs where everyone else can read it except our selves.

The Last Call

Wives, submit yourselves unto your own husbands as unto the Lord (Epj.5:22). This is tough on us, girls, because another version employ the words **be submissive** and **adapt yourselves** and any old thesaurus gives us ten or more words describing the attributes of adaptability:

> Acclimatize accommodate adjust apply compliant docile
> easily led fit habituate harmonize influenceable manageable
> receptive responsive shape taylor yielding

Fortunately for us the verse quoted refers specifically to our *own husbands,* and other men are therefore excluded!

However, an analogy may provide a clear picture to wonderful, caring husbands:

Think of an extraordinarily beautiful pullover. Knitted by hand with painstaking, meticulous, loving care. Stitch by stitch to measured perfection, yours only. An exclusive, unique gift, no duplicates made for anyone else ever. A work of art created by your best Friend and, delivered personally.

What do you think of a gesture of love such as this? In addition, what are you going to do with this exceptional gift?

Will you treasure it as something very special, delighting in its colour and composition, or will you regard it as just another commonplace article, treating it with such non-committal carelessness that it loses shape? Will you perhaps have your dogs play tug-o-war with it, even mess on it? Will you regard it with such indifference that it lands in a pool of mud? Do you cherish it as your favourite garment the more you wear it threadbare?

Think! You take it off with rising temperatures, and snuggle in it when cold. It clings to every curve of your body when you most need it; pliable, ever ready to stretch to its limit. Poor, worn, willing pullover!

It has heard your breathings, your lamentations, covered your moods, your anger, it shook together with your own shaking frame in fear and in laughter. You have had it patched and darned, (the bills were worth it) and, still it welcomes you into its folds. It even smells of you.

Gentle suds, gentle washing by hand and you can slip it on when the tears have dried … A yielding, pliable, reliable garment. Always ready, always waiting … Irreplaceable, unequalled, only one of her kind.

Oh, come on, men! Take another long, hard look at what happened in the Garden and adjust your thinking. And know this: what Adam did, or did not do, still holds dire consequences for all men today, for the individual, and more so for the Church.

Ask why Adam's part in this catastrophic event has gone by with less frankness, and more derogatory emphasis on Eve as temptress and culprit? The Boy's Club, boys! How many 'jokes' have been cracked around Genesis 2 and 3? We need answers here, because through centuries the same approach to the happenings in the Garden of Eden have become rooted in minds—and minds must be renewed if release and healing are to be effected and retained.

Why is it that this snatch out of the Biblical pages of history has always been interpreted in the same way and this fact in itself not been recognized as the most devious and calculated machinations Satan has deployed against man? No unprejudiced scrutiny, no downright, honest repentance! Why?

For the husband is the head of the wife, even as Christ is the head of the church: and he is the saviour of the body.

Therefore as the church is subject unto Christ, so let the wives be to their own husbands in every thing.

Husbands, love your wives, even as Christ also loved the church, and gave himself for it:

That he might sanctify and cleanse it with the washing of water by the word,

That he might present it to himself a glorious church, not having spot or wrinkle, or any such thing; hut that it should be holy and without blemish.

So ought men to love their wives as their own bodies. He that loveth his wife loveth himself.

For no man ever yet hated his own flesh, but nourisheth and cherisheth it, even as the Lord the church;

For this cause shall a man leave his father and mother, and shall be joined unto his wife, and they two shall ne one flesh.

This is a great mystery but I speak concerning Christ and the church.

Nevertheless let every one of you in particular so love his wife even as himself; and the wife see that she reverence his husband. (Eph.5:22-33).

The Curtain Raises

Gen.1:26-28 and *Eph.5.22-23* have repeatedly been coupled together, threshed out, sifted, hammered on, repudiated, used as yardstick, as whip. It has probably been the material provided for the most distorted quip ever toasted at stag parties. And still no change in mindset. The revealed mystery of *Eph.5:32* do not have the prominent place in teaching it deserves; perhaps the profoundness not fully grasped?

And the rib, which the Lord God had taken from man, made he a woman, and brought her unto the man (Gen.2:22).

If a married couple miss the point here, then they have missed the most crucial understanding of the intents and purposes of God for man.

God is so pleased with the man He created in His image and likeness, He thinks so highly of him, that He prepares him an exceptional compliment, and you may use either an e or an I; both are appropriate. He brings a special gift for a special person and the card on the parcel reads:

> To my son Adam,
> With much love,
> from
> Your Father God.

He then delivers the gift personally: AND BROUGHT HER TO THE MAN

5

GOD'S GIFT

The Real Eve

She is a vessel of rare beauty. The contents of this vessel having incomparable qualities and—**all to be poured back into Adam.**

The hands of Yahweh built her to fill Adam to complete wholeness; and ultimately this means a man walking and talking with God.

Only then is her divine purpose fulfilled and is, for Eve, her 'mission achieved.'

Adam and Eve replenished the earth with their own kind only after the fall. Nevertheless, Eve became wholesomely whole and completed when she reproduced, although their progeny were not of the same spiritual composition as their parents had enjoyed before the fall.

She understood the principle of submission instinctively before the Fall, but so did Adam, and neither could say they did not know what God expected of them.

Any God-fearing man who walks in committed surrender and obedience does not need to be taught this principle—his humility is that genuine. He knows it is not a cloak he can fling on at random. Genuine humility is both earned and bestowed. He does not argue about submitting.

Eve willingly empties herself to fill him, thus bringing forth the best in both. She has the wisdom to know that in yielding lays great power. It bears the fruit of righteousness and the stamp of spiritual maturity of the highest degree. All of this is the manna, the daily stuff her brood feeds on.

Any other course for Eve is an unnatural one. She does not fit into any other role. Deep within she knows she is to complete her man, not compete with him, and in completing her husband, she knows her true Husband directly favours her. She disciplines herself towards the intents and purposes of her great God with a clear understanding of her *perfectly* perfect role.

Godly Wisdom

Eve blooms when Adam avails himself of her phenomenal equipment as crutch, as nutriment and as radar. He *earns* her respect and fails miserably when he demands it. Obviously the spirit, soul and body of Adam are alone and incomplete without the qualities of his helper-meet, but pride of life will rob Adam of totality should he refute her abilities.

If Adam is gifted with Godly wisdom, he will let the Holy Spirit teach him to guard the qualities keeping him filled and fitted. He will not trample underfoot with inconsideration or selfishness the offerings she contributes. His godly wife's obedience to the Father's requirements, he knows, are not his to demand for himself, but is honoured, maintained and sustained by God Himself, and in full cycle is poured back into his own being—a true man of God. In other words, he will go cautiously and not shoot himself in the foot.

Her very willingness to submit her gifts and meet him voluntarily with help and support should not become a beautiful thing degraded and warped by his manipulations. Control is not easily detected in its first stages. The deeper a certain type of personality gets hooked into this stratagem the more difficult it is to extricate him self should he eventually recognize the condition.

Tactful but firm resistance and an open verbal approach may come as an eye-opener and a surprise to some offenders. Sensible discussion of controlling tendencies is a big plus but unfortunately never successful where one party is either unapproachable, un-teachable, prone to unreasonable anger, or both permit themselves to be drawn into futile argument. We must be honest and admit that controlling women not only abound, but their ploys are degrading and despicable to say the least.

In the initial stages a controller acts blind to what he is inflicting and derives pleasure from exerting his power. He regards it as his right. He explains away his conduct with every reason but the truth. Eventually he will not relinquish the soul-force he is imposing: a streak of sadism and secret satisfaction with what he is doing to his 'victim' creeps in and not even in rare moments of honesty will he admit to his conduct. We may certainly raise the subject of evil spirits at work.

Secondly, his unregenerate associates can't or won't help. They see the sick of his traits, see the consequences, cannot discern the demonic origin, avoid involvement, and lack genuine concern for those who are victimized.

The bartender may hear the crude jokes and see the shaking heads. The church may extend a measure of solace in counselling, and encouragement to attend 'another excellent course, see if you can get your wives or your husbands to come as well. Your names should be in by next Thursday and it costs only R100 per person. The speaker is a well-known exponent on the subject of matrimony and you will really enjoy it. This is a must!'

Thirdly: when Adam took the fruit from Eve of his own free choice, he was a dead duck. For men it was a sell-out.

6

UNLESS THEY BE AGREED

Zaccheus

Over thousands of years males have restricted themselves with a false concept of dominance. Adam had forfeited his open walk with God and man. What he did to Eve has left the male gender drained and dry. It has sucked from them the ability to open up to their wives in honest, surrendered fellowship. They cannot unfold, sob their pain and misery, and be comforted.

Webster's definition of fellowship is: 'one of a pair (fellow) suited for one another, companions, partners.' Few men talk without reserve in the close privacy of their bedrooms. They uphold the rigidity of their boyhood: 'cry-baby, cry! Sissy!'

Neither will they cry to God for they are not in fellowship with Him: the Holiest of Holies is the place of togetherness, and some men will not enter. They are held captive by an influence shutting them out and closing them up, desperately sewing fig leaves to cover their nakedness. This foreign power will not have them breaking into tears before fellow believers, or breaking before God in surrender.

Who, or what, is this influence holding men captive?

Escapism bears bitter fruit and if a husband turns to males-only for release, good. Fine. The release may last for a spell, but he will inevitably burn his fingers. Be well advised to carefully first investigate the origin and subversive intentions of males-only movements, for these pyramids are built on sand. Do not be misled and inveigled by surface integrity and 'togetherness with men' who are bonding and building toward the 're-establishment of males as undisputed, absolute head' for male superiority is another masked religion riding on the back of the golden calf, and might well be named Idolatry. .

The 'fellowshipping of the brotherhood' is a dangerous grey area, looking and sounding so good, but one may well be led up the garden path by quasi-spirituality. It would be wasting precious time in a dangerous cul-de-sac. As soon as the tendency of a gathering or movement to *evade doctrinal distinctions* is detected, remove yourself. Quicker still if you are pressed to make compromises concerning Truth and error, for the only way to go is the Way indicated by the Blood of Jesus. Error can be so inviting, convincing and persuasive. With evil hidden yet operating, one could be made to feel you are an obstruction in the way of progress and solutions for the dilemmas of our time. It doesn't work that way. Dissociate yourself from male self-righteousness. Godliness cannot be obtained through membership of organizations and unity with other men. Bond with your wife. Go wash your pullover in gentle suds, get your own hands clean in the process, dry it tenderly, put it on and snuggle. Do not find out too late you have misappropriated your gift from God.

Consider *Luk.19*. Zaccheus is the literal description of a little man who enriches himself at the expense of others. Of course, being a small individual, he cannot see Jesus in the crowd, let alone discern the Majesty of His Person.

Zaccheus may well have been of the type who MUST have some supportive structure or system to lift him out of, and above the ordinary people around him. He does not even know this. Because he feels rejected and insecure he MUST always be one step ahead, in the highest position, compensating for the hostility and spurn his personality and profession evokes. Therefore, his compulsive need is to keep running ahead of those moving on—it would seem in this particular case the crowd was moving on with Jesus—

But Jesus already knows all about him.

Zaccheus conveniently scales up the highest and the right, the best, and the only tree, for he MUST always sit in the better vantage point. Is this the way he has always sung his spiel? Even in the privacy of his home?

But perhaps we should give Zaccheus the benefit of the doubt for he really took pains to see the famous Master. Can be he did not think of asking himself why he wanted to? Did he suffer some inner turmoil; did he not perhaps begin to realize the futility of his efforts at being higher, bigger and better than he actually was? Perhaps, if he could see Jesus clearly, something of all he'd heard about the Man would rub off on him! No harm in trying ...

For sure, he would not miss anything and here was the Man of the Moment coming his way! Neither would he mix with the mob but at the same time, he would not be without the juicy titbits. What a predicament! Jesus was in the crowd, and he could not see Jesus for the crowd!

But the King of kings was not going to have that small mean man looking down upon Him from a place other than actual, existing conditions. Zaccheus must come down from his structure, without his handful of chosen buddies, without his seasonal ticket to the rugby, without his tankard of beer, without the support of his chosen perch, down, down, down. Back to earth. Stand on firm, level ground. Face-to-face, eye-to-eye, be inexorably confronted with Divine Love.

The opportunity of a lifetime! Hurry, Zaccheus! The Sovereign, stopping by a mere man, a damnable tax collector, a sinner! Do not delay!

'Hurry and come down, for I must today stay with you at your house where I know I shall also find your wife, your children, your home, your heart!'

And he made haste, and came down, and received him joyfully .And when they saw it, they all murmured saying, That he was gone to be guest with a man that is a sinner.(Luk.19:1-7).

When Zaccheus welcomed Jesus into his home, he was faced with another predicament: the muttering of other people, the people whom he had slighted and fleeced before; and those people whose favour once he had sought.

Don't worry, friend, this condition is nothing new—when you begin heeding the Master's voice, people around you begin squirming—

But having come down to earth and facing Jesus, a shift in heart and thinking takes place and understanding is birthed in the inner man. What a discovery! HER SUBMISSION TO ME IS GOD'S PROPERTY—NOT MINE!

And new life flows into home and marriage!

Walking In Newness

If a wife is by rebirth a seriously committed saint, then she has been baptized into Jesus Christ and therefore baptized into His death. She is IN Christ, meaning that the Indwelling Christ is on His rightful throne within her. And this means she has Another Person indwelling Who alone has full rights.

As a completed (reborn) child of the Father, she has no rights to claim as her own. But neither do you, nor I, Christian believers or not. No one may usurp the place of Christ in the life of another with demands to suit personal, preconceived conclusions and conveniences either by suppression, manipulation, subversive control, domination, religion or influence of any other description.

Know ye not, that so many of us were baptized into Jesus Christ were baptized into His death?

Therefore we are buried with him by baptism into death: that like as Christ was raised up from the dead by the glory of the Father; even so we also should walk in new-ness of life (Rom.6:3,4).

Paul is not talking here about the christening font or baptism by immersion, but immersion in Christ. Do you have a dead wife? Oh man! For the sake of Jesus, she constantly is being handed over to death so the resurrection life of Jesus may be evidenced! We are talking about a wife that is supernaturally raised, ALIVE!

Ever heard of stumbling blocks? Know what the Bible says about them? Find out, for God is the protector of new Eve and He is not to be toyed with.

If a husband is clever enough to detect Satan's undermining manoeuvres, he is to stick to personal obedience to God's precepts and discard his own concept of wifely submission. Tactless suppression of a woman's emotions with isolated verses of Scripture is valuable ground lost to the enemy.

Paul is the one most quoted when it comes to women. Do not use him as a trump card and confront an angry or hurting female with, for instance, *Eph.5:22*, or *Col.3:18*.

If the husband knows anything about prayer, then perhaps he should become a 'remembrancer.' *Which shall never hold their peace day or night: 'ye that make mention of the Lord, keep not silence.*

And give him no rest till he establish, and till he make Jerusalem a praise in the earth (Is.62:7).

Remind Father God you know *1 Pet.3:7* is conditional. *Likewise, ye husbands, dwell with them according to knowledge, giving honour unto the wife, as unto the weaker vessel, and as being heirs together of the grace of life; that your prayers not be hindered.*

A Remembrancer

Husband, stand in the place where Adam should have been. Intercede for your wife; remind Father that punishment of woman, because of the disobedience of the first woman, has been borne by His Son. Husband, do you heed the Holy Spirit when He prompts you to remind God of His forgiveness through Jesus, and even more so when she suffers the pangs of physical childbirth? *Gen.3:16?*

Primarily, the husband has spiritual responsibilities toward his wife and family, not rights because he is the head. He cannot take a superior position for granted. His place as head is often, all too often, unpleasant and painful, sacrificial, and calls him to having a servant heart at the expense of his own person. He has to give of himself to the point of breaking—the reward and the glory lie in the beyond of now; a crown to place again at the feet of Jesus.

If he is in any sense desperate, at his wits' end, he can be sure of God reaching out to him without preamble on his part. He does not need to know anything about prayer, but that God is sovereign and he has Jesus on the right hand of the Throne interceding for him, deserving or not.

On occasion I have sensed that the more a husband is perplexed by his non-pliable, grating wife, the more desperate and merciless he becomes—yet all the more God loves him just as he is. His pent-up anger and frustration and disap-pointment at having saddled himself with an unfortunate alliance rules his dispo-sition and emotions, but the deeper his misery, the higher the Lord places him on His list of priorities, and the closer the Presence of Jesus surrounds him. If he but knew this. If he but understood.

Please, dear husband, do not use 'the church' and 'God's order' and 'wifely submission' as a crutch to support ego trips and bidding physical needs. Unclasp those clutching fingers and 'rafa' all dominance yelling its head off for appease-ment. ('rafa' means:: *to cause to let fall that which hinders*).

What we willingly let go of, God gives back to us. Through Him the husband will find his status and stature returned, clothed in quiet understanding, carrying with it a calm, reserved dignity, simply and wordlessly expressed in a certain qual-ity of authority and inner strength that will have his woman yielding her love in support and admiration—*those* are the qualities women acknowledge. To *those* attributes they back down, calmed, safe, and secure. *Then* he has all the respect, the trust, and all the willing, serving love. *This* makes women say: What a man!

There is a woman behind every man. And there is a reason behind every nag-ging woman.

7

THE SAGA OF ADAM AND EVE

Not Without Effort

We know the story of Adam and Eve has much to teach, and many believers take Genesis (or the whole Bible) literally, but as many also look for an acceptable reason behind the meaning ...

We confess God's Word to be the Truth; let us therefore tremble for in any degree of carnality, we can overstep and use Scriptures to say anything *we* want to say. None have immediate knowledge of a mystery, or perception of something, without putting in a little effort, and prejudices harboured will hinder comprehension.

And so it is written: The first man Adam was made a living soul; the last Adam was made a quickening spirit.

Howbeit that was not first which is spiritual, but that which is natural, and afterward that which is spiritual.

The first man is of the earth, earthy, the second man is the Lord from heaven.

As is the earth, which are they also that are earthy; and as is the heavenly, such are they also that are heavenly (1 Cor.15:45-48).

These verses show Adam as being earthy, natural, a living soul.

Genesis tells us they (Adam and Eve) were made in the image and likeness of God, Who is Spirit. This then adds spirit to Adam and Eve. The *'breath of life'* *(Gen.2:7)*, which the Creator breathed into man, is not to be confused with His Holy Spirit.

These passages put together indicate Adam and Eve as being capable of communicating with God and settles it finally: they were created spirit, soul and body *(1 Thes.5:23)*.

Added to the above, and according to *Gen. 1 and 2*, God had also equipped Adam and Eve with sound reasoning powers, without which they certainly could not have met His command to exercise dominion. They were, therefore, decision-making human beings for no one can possibly subdue the earth without a measure of reason functioning.

Adam and Eve had no need to know the difference between good and evil, (blessing and calamity) *(Gen.3:5)* because they were created to be totally reliant on their Creator, their wills fused and entirely within His.

When first man and woman could see the difference between good and evil, when they tasted of this knowledge, they comprehended that they had power. They could exercise their own will for now they had acquired a frame of reference for every choice and decision, thus enabling them to steer their own lives. They did not need their Creator any longer to do it for them.

The predicament and the responsibility and the results for man lies in the moment when he decides and makes his own choices, and *this is the stark consequence of knowing.* He plays god over his own life; he exalts himself and declares his independence. He is in rebellion against his Creator and as punishment he will walk in the dark, unless he comes to his senses and repent.

Because God is the Creator of good and evil, light and dark, prosperity and calamity, **He is also the only One in command of it**. He should direct our decision-making and the results are to flow forth from His omniscient heart alone—if we pray 'Thy will be done' then we should mean exactly that! But with our childlike trust tainted, we take over and make a mess of everything.

Adam and Eve were equipped to hear His voice and His directions, to implement His guidance and instructions, to meet with Him in every area of their existence, and to accomplish His desires. It was expected of them to be completely dependent on Him; and in turn they would be the recipients of everything they could ever need. They could meet with Him in the cool of the day and fellowship God-consciously without the barrier of self-consciousness.

What God wanted was their obedience, undivided loyalty, their adoring love and worship—**then He would provide all and do all**—and His conditions have never changed.

We have lost those privileges—and then regained them, for the Son has reconciled us with the Father at great cost. But no, oh no! We are bent on doing our own thing and do not heed the meaning behind the meaning of the seventh day of rest *(Heb.4:6-11)*, being so occupied with an external expression of *Ex.20:8*, that we are not resting in Him to complete the choices and the decisions He wants to make in His own time through us.

The first couple was commanded to be fruitful, to multiply, to fill the earth and subdue it (with all its vast resources); and have dominion over all *(Gen.1:28)*.

This tremendous task calls for an ability to distinguish between what is right and what is not so right; of differentiating, deciding between the yes's and the no's, coming to satisfactory conclusions. This is evident from the Biblical accounts of the first man and his woman, *Ish* and *Isha*, before they transgressed.

There is with human beings a strong tendency to disregard the obvious: God does not expect us to do what He knows we cannot handle. If He has equipped us for a task, then He expects our trust and obedience in the matter. We may, therefore, safely contend that Adam could reason clearly with God, with himself, with Eve, and—YES, with the serpent.

Contrary to the generally accepted opinion through the ages, Scriptural accounts indicate strongly that Adam knew what business he was about in the Garden of Eden and, **he knew what he was doing when he took the fruit from Eve and ate.**

To make a further thought-provoking statement: the serpent was already in the Garden *(Ezek. 8:12* and relevant Scriptures support) when Adam appeared on the scene or God would not have instructed him not to toy with the knowledge of good and evil—that brilliant evil being lay awaiting his opportunity, coiled and ready to strike.

Eve could hear the serpent communicating and so could Adam. They had the same faculties and the same powers of reasoning.

Using different translations, we read that Adam was by her side (or, with her) when she took the fruit and ate.

But Eve definitely was the first to give shape and action to what she was hearing—and Adam listened—

One can almost hear his rationalizing. What Eve and the serpent were talking about sounded so good! Almost the same as his God and best Friend had said, and Who had warned him neither to touch nor eat of that one particular tree! He'd wondered about the tree, had he not been put in the garden to dress and tend trees? But now, did God mean he couldn't even approach the middle of the garden, or broach the subject? Surely, wasn't this before *Wo-man* was made? A time back?

Once you start reasoning things out for yourself, the flesh flashes into position and possession. For a split second, in part, or completely, you will always think of yourself first and what the situation holds for you at best.

Listen, fellow saints! Whether you be the first man or the last one, whether you be innocent, or merely an earth-minded person, alive yet dead with an unquickened spirit, heathen or Christian, whether you are reborn and Spirit-filled or not, SATAN DOES NOT CARE TWO HOOTS WHO OR WHAT YOU

ARE. Given the slightest chance, he will use every trick in the book, every available opportunity, to plant his lies in whatever type of soil at hand. The seed he has sown may lie dormant for an indefinite period, but what you *do* with thoughts that crop up, will *always* be a determinant factor in your life.

Adam and Eve were no exception. In spite of their close walk with God, they became the first human beings hooked by what had every appearance of being sensible truth.

This is the point where Adam slipped up.

Instead of quashing the whole thing immediately, he joined the gang. Surely knowing how to live by your own independent laws could not be that dangerous or bad!

Let us follow the chronological course of events. The serpent's approach is shrewd and calculated. He chooses Eve.

Why Eve?

Now the serpent was more subtil than any beast of the field which the Lord God had made. And he said unto the woman, Yea, hath God said, Ye shall not eat of every tree of the garden? (Gen.3:1)

The root word of the Hebrew for serpent means 'a brilliant being that charms by suggestions and whisperings to the mind.' Ah! Now we come to evil stuff! The strategy at the time, and always since, has been to stimulate and foment thinking—based on all but the full truth—and partial truth is as valid a gap as any other. The serpent took it.

And the woman said unto the serpent, We may eat of the fruit of the trees of the garden,

But of the fruit of the tree which is in the midst of the garden God hath said, Ye shall not eat of it, neither shall ye touch it, lest ye die (Gen.3:2,3).

Not so abstract—her answer is plain and simple. 'We will die if we eat of it.' Note: Eve uses the plural we. Interesting. This means Adam had indeed informed her of God's command that 'We are not to eat or touch of the fruit of the tree in the midst of the garden, lest we die.' Adams's words, or Eve's interpretation of Adam's words? We do not read that God had addressed Eve on the matter before she ate.

In reply to the serpent, Eve omits the crucial words 'of the knowledge of good and evil' that do not refer to anything physical, but the intangible. Did Eve perhaps understand that the fruit was poisonous and therefore caused physical death? *(Gen.2:16,17)*

THE SERPENT KNEW ALL OF THIS. HE KNEW EXACTLY WHAT HE WAS DOING.

However, Eve did not utter 'of the knowledge of good and evil.' Why?

Dare we say: she added the vital words by implication? This makes the difference and determines our choice of opinion. What is the Holy Spirit saying here?

Did the serpent choose Eve because she was incorrectly or only partially informed?

Consider the major upheavals, the factions and divisions caused by differing points of view. Consider the endless examination and cross-examination of words, sentences, passages and whole chapters and Books. Consider the writings that made the canon and those left out of it, the countless teachings, the time and finance spent on research, angry bickering and intellectual feuds. Then feel free to change your mind if you so wish when you reconsider the drama of Adam and Eve along the lines of human behaviour. It will be a very good thing if this raises further dispute—it may bring people to look afresh at the first recorded abuse of Woman.

Had Adam but fully enlightened Eve, just those few missing yet revealing words, the serpent would not have been able to spring his surprise on her.

Ask the question: if, had Adam in those moments but availed himself of Eve's spiritual abilities, would he not have enjoyed indispensable support from his wife in ousting the serpent and thus maintaining their dominion?

Either Adam refrained from telling Eve what the deadly fruit embraced and she was genuinely unaware of danger, or the original interpreters and translators did not bother to repeat the few important words. *Or Eve was a downright liar even before she took and ate.*

If early legendary accounts by word of mouth excluded the words, then certainly the grossest injustice ever has been committed against Man.

Why have expounders through the years ignored this? God says: *Thy first father hath sinned, and thy teachers have transgressed against me (Is.43:27)*. This verse refers to the fall of Adam. It also refers to Jacob, to Hebrew teachers, to false teachers, to interpreters, and this same verse cannot be more lucid: a lie has been perpetrated, cleverly infiltrated, and kept going.

What is the real issue here? The controversy and the main line of the present debate, is that the omission of these few words indicate grave offence. It has given rise to misunderstanding, much misery, and it constitutes the philosophy upon which the male gender has built its assumptive dominance. Satan had successfully laid the foundation stones of his first stronghold in Man.

Assist me in unravelling above statements for the thrust of this whole book is not against overstepping individuals and disabled partners, but, as seen in the bigger, timeless scheme of things, against a stronghold—a subtle, pervasive force restricting the male gender with a misconception of headship, ruling and true leadership, and his marching out of step with his Creator.

The Lie

In reading these verses carefully, one has strong evidence of Eve not being aware of spiritual danger; the serpent was the first to impart details, however twisted, and nowhere do we read of God speaking to the woman He had made, except after the fatal eating.

Was she misinformed, or not adequately warned by Adam, even if unwittingly so on his part? If so, then Eve certainly was the one most vulnerable and open to deception. Like us—Adam probably never gave the warning another thought. It seems so far fetched; we sometimes just don't bother to give our partners full details. Familiar?

Yet, this was the one weak, unguarded spot, and, the serpent took the gap. As he always does.

And the serpent said unto the woman, Ye shall not surely die: for God doth know that in the day ye eat thereof, then your eyes shall be opened, and ye shall be as gods, knowing good and evil.

And when the woman saw that the tree was good for food, and that it was pleasant to the eyes, and a tree to be desired to make one wise, she took of the fruit thereof, and did eat, and gave also unto her husband with her, and he did eat (Gen.3:4-6)

Let us be easy on Adam, and not give his wife any opportunity to abscond. Presently we shall look for, and find her, in today's Eve. But we should first probe a few misconceptions continually cropping up.

Did Eve coerce, deceive or tempt Adam? Categorically no. This is neither stated nor even vaguely suggested in Genesis. It should rather be asked what lay on innocent Adam's mind when the serpent roused innocent Eve to a discussion of the potential knowledge, for he was with her.

Did Adam of his own volition take from Eve and eat? Yes. One cannot but sense a reproach to God when he admits later in *verse 12: the woman whom Thou gavest me gave me of the tree and I did eat.* 'You see, my Father, if you hadn't given her to me I would not now be in this pickle …'

If he did not want to eat, he would not have taken. He would have said: 'No, thank you'.

Job 31:33 hits the nail on the head: *If I covered my transgressions as Adam, by hiding mine iniquity in mine bosom …*

And *James 1:14,15* gives us the 'how' it is done: *but every man is tempted when he is drawn away of his own lust and enticed. Then when lust hath conceived it bringeth forth sin, and sin, when it is finished, bringeth forth death.*

And did Adam know before Eve was even made that the forbidden tree held knowledge of good and evil? Yes. He had the full truth plus a direct forbidding command from God. Adam had no excuse for eating.

Our first response to sin committed is blaming everything and everyone else but one's self. No fancy name for it: the sin of self-deception. It immediately sank its vile fangs deep into the flesh of Man.

As always, one sin leads to another, and another, and another. Adam was the first to feel this law cut to the quick. We, coming after him, follow his ways—follow my leader—unless of course we cast ourselves betimes onto Second Adam to come and salvage the messy bits and pieces, entreating Him to restore.

God created the first man consistent with His own character. Yet, strange as it may seem, innocent Adam proved himself questionable on a good number of things. How can this be?

Firstly, rebellion. Many expounders reason that rebellion came because of the fall. Not so. Adam was already in rebellion when he lifted his hand to take and eat, or he would not have done so. He had received the command not to eat, had he not? How much effort did Eve put into her persuasive voice? Not much, one can guess, because rebellion occurs when suppressed thoughts build up to words and action. Adam was deceiving himself. You cannot attempt deceiving God and think the devil is not interested. He himself had rebelled and knew all about falling. If permitted, he would lead every human being, enticed by lies and half-truths, into rebellion.

Now, at this point, there comes from God a thrust of truth for Adam; always a severe test for any man who knows he has landed himself in trouble. Adam therefore had several choices:

Would he give himself for his bride by taking the blame?

Would he confess his neglected responsibility and his disobedience?

Would he confess curiosity and repent of his ambitious hunger for the knowledge of good and evil, which God had prohibited much earlier and had lain dormant in his bosom?

Would he intercede and throw himself and his beautiful, erring, misguided spouse on the generous, forgiving love of his Father?

He did none of these.

Now hear it, folks. What Adam missed in those cataclysmic moments, present-day Adam is still missing!! Job had spotted it centuries later and said it so simply: it lay in the bosom!

Adam could not say No! to the eating and Abram could not say No! to another kind of eating. Eve and Sarai had both walked into the same Satanic snare. They, all of them, knew they were in forbidden territory—and did not let God have His way with them.

When God challenges Adam, he takes the most obvious and the most convenient gap, just as the serpent had done: Eve.

Adam simply expunges his guilt by refocusing it on Eve.

Eve, Eve! Poor, poor Eve! The very first woman abused by her husband. He did not take responsibility for his own decision to eat. He did not guard her. Nor did he guide her. He took full advantage of her eating to satisfy his own want. He took, he ate.

He could, or should, have said: 'No, my darling wife, don't. You are not to respond to these whisperings. These are deceiving thoughts. For God Himself told me, and now I am telling you, we will not eat of this deadly fruit. Serpent! I command you to get out of here!'

He had dominion, and the serpent was subject to him. He had God-given authority to repel and oust the serpent. He did not even rebuke it. Satan had laid the foundations of yet another stronghold (2 Cor. 10:3-5).

When a man, such as Adam, and Abram, and any other man for that matter, receive a direct word from God, he is not to confer with flesh and blood. He is to stick to clear-cut, straightforward obedience; mindful of God always having sound reasons for a command.

Adam did not protect his wife from the deceiving spirit. He failed in quality of leadership. He did not walk and relate in full truth with his wife. Nor did he stand fast to hold the ground given him by God. He thought of his own eating and to this day still comes off best where Eve is concerned. The fruit was good to the taste, but bitter after the swallow. And to this day, if man is not in his Redeemer, the serpent is still in Adam's Eden, and so retains the better of him, for Adam had lost himself. And he had lost his Eve. He had lost his God. But he has not lost the serpent.

The inevitable came—the confrontation. In addition, for sure, the all too familiar selfish bickering that accompanies every move of the ever-present flesh. And don't we all know it—the sick, disgusted feeling when you have irrevocably let something precious slip from your fingers because of selfish stupidity and you know you have to face the consequences!

With our Heavenly Father, consequences are not necessarily irredeemable. He will hear us out, and help, but then we have to be honest with Him. God came walking in the garden in the cool of the day and Adam and his wife hid themselves from the presence of the Lord God amongst the trees of the garden.

Still In Hiding

This was summary jurisdiction. The sentences were severe, worse than abrupt execution. The Most High was in no mood for blessings and the punishment for Eve was akin to a curse. Suffice it so say, God was angry. Because he was made first, and therefore accountable, it is the man God calls.

And the Lord God called unto Adam and said unto him, Where art thou? (Gen.3:8).

Where are you, Adam? Profound.

"I'm hiding from you, God! Even today I'm still hiding, Father God. My fig leaf is a façade, a sham, and I'm hoping Eve will never come up to seeing me for what I am, and for what I did to her!'

'I don't want to see myself either, and oh my God, not any other man, not the serpent, nor You, must ever make me look at myself! I don't want to see myself. Don't you understand, Father, all of this is really her fault! I told her we'll die but I didn't feel to need bother looking after her all the time. Communication and explanations is a bore. I don't have to be hearing her, do I? And I am not going to be held responsible for her. Anyway, it's all because of her insubmission, God, she just doesn't listen to me—oh, where can I find a few more fig leaves?'

This verse, as found in another translation, is quite shattering: *If like Adam or like other men I have concealed my transgressions by hiding my iniquity in my bosom (.Job 31:33).*

Whence does evil come? If it was not created, how then did it evolve? We persist in calling Adam 'good' before the fall. This is contradictory to Jesus commenting *Why callest thou me good? There is none good but one that is God (Matt.19:17).*

In the beginning was the Word, and the Word was with God, and the Word was God.

The same was in the beginning with God.

All things were made by him; and without him was not any thing made that was made. (Joh.1:1-3).

I am the Lord, and there is none else, there is no God beside me; I girded thee, though thou hast not known me. That they may know from the rising of the sun and from the west, that there is none beside me. I am the Lord and there is none else.

I form the light, and create darkness: I make peace, and create evil; I the Lord do all these things.

Drop down, ye heavens, from above, and let the skies pour down righteousness: let them bring forth salvation, and let righteousness spring up together: I the Lord have created it (Is.45:5-8).

God says He makes peace and He creates evil. The word '*ra*' has many variants: evil, bad, wicked, distress, misery, calamity and disaster, harm. One translator makes a distinction between moral evil and physical evil.

Pointless warning anyone against something that does not exist, anything that just is not there—God would not have warned Adam specifically against eating fruit from the tree of knowledge of good and evil if it was not already growing luscious fruit in the middle of the Garden. Had Adam not perhaps tended the tree? How must we read this portion of Scripture? What is it saying to us?

May we understand the garden to be representative of the heart, of the whole life, a person's own little piece of world? I'm happy cultivating and dressing my own independent, personal, little laws on what is good and what is a little less than good. And then, of course, living out my own approaches in making my own little garden work out for me. And I am upset if you don't agree and co-operate to have me working for mine only—thus we continually find ourselves in a position where we must choose between Light and Dark.

That musical, harmonious, glittering, beautiful, brilliant Being was in the heart of God when it was created, and it chose to exalt itself against its Creator as did also the man Adam whom He had created in His likeness. Initially the heart produces the offspring; every creation comes out of the heart and thus I was born with God's principles in my heart—yet I was born in sin. All principles channel its creativity through every other man as well, whatever his medium.

Now, this bright Being definitely knew of good and evil when it, for reasons unknown to us, desired independence and came into open rebellion.

(Ezekiel provides detail: *Thou sealest up the sum, full of wisdom, and perfect in beauty (28:12b) Thou hast been in Eden, the garden of God; (13a) Thou art the anointed cherub that covereth; and I have set thee so: thou wast upon the holy mountain of God; thou hast walked up and down in the midst of the stones of fire (:14) Thou wast perfect in thy ways from the day that thou wast created, till iniquity was found in thee (:15) Your heart was proud and lifted up because of your beauty; you corrupted your wisdom for the sake of your splendour. I cast you to the ground (Ezek.28:17).*

Connect Ezekiel and Isaiah, where both prophets describe Satan, and man, in rebellion. Self-serving forms the basis to five luring areas in which 'I will' challenges are flung at God, with pride and rebellion leeching on each other, and it boils down in simple terms to self-consciousness taking the place of God-consciousness. *How art thou fallen from heaven, Lucifer, son of the morning! How art thou cut down to the ground, which didst weaken the nations! For thou has said in thine heart, I will ascend into heaven, I will exalt my throne above the stars of God: I will sit also upon the mount of the congregation, in the sides of the north; I will ascend above the heights of the clouds: I will be like the most High (Is.14:12-14)*

And Jesus: *said unto them, I beheld Satan as lightning fall from heaven (Luk.10:18)).*

Therefore evil, as created by God, does exist. To make a direct, unconditional statement: Evil it is growing right in the middle of my garden (my heart), and bearing delectable fruit. **My business is not to eat nor even touch of it. It is a vital matter of obedience, of knowing my position of authority in Christ, and of making the right choices.**

There is no need for us to question God's wisdom in creating darkness and evil, for God is sovereign. Omniscient, omnipotent God, in promoting His ends and purposes, even hardens the heart of whomever He wishes *(Rom.9:17-23).*

However, we cannot afford ignorance. Knowledge about the enemy's wiles, snares, and ever active conniving is imperative. Unfortunately, this knowledge comes only through painful experience and astute observation; it is rather pointless to hide our heads in the ground, as does the proverbial ostrich. The ministry of Jesus dealt primarily with disease and demon infestation. They *do* exist.

Forewarned is forearmed—warfare cannot be successfully conducted without having received firsthand intelligence. No shrewd general ever attempts battle without reliable means and a well-considered defence plan *(Eph.6:10-20).*

Do not underestimate this enemy, because he will have informed you that you are not to take him seriously, or you are taking your eyes off Jesus, or you are overdoing your interest in his methods and therefore you are dangerously drawing his attention to your person and setting yourself up as a special target. The Blood of Jesus, the Holy Spirit, personal righteousness, and a healthy balance on the subject of demons will keep us. A sound church will unite in dealing with the adversary, and not accommodate every teacher on demonology and Satanism coming their way, instilling fear of impending evil. Of course the devil would have fear assailing us! Let us rather hold our steadfast stand in full Truth. Continually induced to believe lies, we respond to what we think are our own thoughts. Being tempted is not sin, but it is our participation in what evil offers that God considers as sin; and The Lie has power to inveigle us to tasting and then eating before we even know we have done so! Poo Adam.

Many Scriptures refer to light and darkness and most of these pertain to a right or wrong mindset.

This then is the message which we have heard of him and declare unto you, that God is light, and in him is no darkness at all.

If we say that we have fellowship with him, and walk in darkness, we lie, and do not the truth

But if we walk in the light, as he is in the light, we have fellowship one with another, and the blood of Jesus Christ his Son cleanseth us from all sin.

If we say that we have no sin, we deceive ourselves, and the truth is not in us (1 Joh.1:5,7). These verses are not contradictory to Is.45:7.

The Holy Spirit leads us into fresh scope and sphere when we examine *Eph.5:8-14.* When verse 13 becomes clear, understanding about warfare dawns. If we have no part in any form of darkness then the Light within us rebukes external darkness and exposes it. An unbroken walk in Truth is truly remarkable spiritual warfare.

Keep on depositing the Word into your bank account, putting it in, putting it in. There comes a moment when it takes shape, falls into place, perhaps in a flash of instant understanding. Or a particular Word may get a quiet grip on one's mind; but for sure we will in time receive clarity and be blessed with certainty that a step forward, or more, has been granted.

I cease not to give thanks for you, making mention of you in my prayers

That the God of our Lord Jesus Christ, the Father of glory, may give unto you the spirit of wisdom and revelation in the knowledge of him

The eyes of your understanding being enlightened: that ye may know what is the hope of his calling, and what the riches of the glory of his inheritance in the saints (Eph.1:16-18).

8

WITH GOD WATCHING ON

The Verdict

And Eve? She does not fare well at all. As the most suitable target she now finds herself a'twixt the devil and the man, with God watching on.

He that covereth his sins shall not prosper: but whosoever confesseth and forsaketh them shall have mercy (Prov.28:13).

Had Adam but instantly repented! Had he but immediately interceded for his bride!

And the Lord God said unto the woman, What is this that thou hast done? And the woman said, The serpent beguiled me, and I did eat.

And the Lord God said unto the serpent, Because thou hast done this, thou art cursed above all cattle, and above every beast of the field, upon thy belly shalt thou go, and dust shalt thou eat all the days of thy life:

And I will put enmity between thy seed and her seed; it shall bruise thy head, and thou shall bruise his heel.

Unto the woman he said: I will greatly multiply thy sorrow and thy conception; in sorrow thou shall bring forth children; and thy desire shall be to thy husband, and he shall rule over thee (Gen.3:13-16).

Genesis 3:16! A verse containing so much that without the Holy Spirit we cannot come anywhere near full comprehension of all it implies.

Two important principles though, stand out starkly and are either overlooked, or deliberately ignored. Only a small handful of saints, who have the eye and the ear, will take cognisance and apply or teach the principles contained therein.

Two Principles Ignored

Firstly: No court of law will pass judgment and convict any person before he has committed a crime.

Eve received her sentence (punishment) *after* she had transgressed *and not before*. Therefore, when she was made, God did not place on her any of the disabling restrictions as given in Gen.3:16. He did not pass judgement, nor did He curse her when He brought her to Adam the man. *God did not even address Eve.* **Gen.3:16 is not a fundamental law but is punishment for disobedience.**

THE PUNISHMENT WAS LIFTED WHEN THE BLOOD OF JESUS WROUGHT FORGIVENESS AND RECONCILIATION. Redemption covers the past, the present and the future. Tetelestai. *'It is done.'* An accomplished fact.

The contents and implications of Gen.3:16 were not God's original plan and purpose for Eve. His will and pleasure was for her to meet Adam willingly with help. He was made first, she was brought to him as part of himself, he was responsible for both of them as much as he would have been for only himself before she was added to him, although the same standard and set of moral rules would apply to each. There will be no distinctions made when finally they stand before the judgement seat of God.

Adam would be head, guide, and protector of her as unto his own bones and flesh, walking in unity and in dominion, subduing the earth *together*. As one, as does Christ unto His own body, the Church, whose spirit corporate is His future Bride.

God has fulfilled His promise to all of woman: our Saviour has paid the full price for her sin. It is man himself who holds against Eve the transgression in the Garden, not God. **Man himself has made a law of Eve's punishment**.

The promise of the Seed of woman has been fulfilled. Verse 15 proclaims a just God putting His Divine remedy to work at once. The instant Eve succumbed to the lies of Satan, the Seed of woman started His journey of atonement down through the ages. The right moment would come—only one Passover in so many centuries—and the head of the Enemy would be bruised. Her punishment was lifted at the Cross when Jesus affirmed: 'It is done.' She is redeemed and Gen.3:16 wiped off her slate. Eve is reinstated.

God knew there could be only one way out. How? Certainly not *1 Tim.2:15*, (taken at face value by the man in the street). This is not the answer. If ever exegesis is a stumbling block, then this is it! Physical childbearing is not a guarantee for salvation; Jesus is the only way. But Satan is doing his utmost to keep the male gender ignorant of the magnificent work of redemption that took place two thousand years ago, and he succeeds in having ignorance and arrogance clinging to perversion of God's original intentions for Eve.

There is no account in Genesis that God created Eve with a desire to be dominated or brought into subjection by the rule of her husband. Again, it is fruit of The Lie when women passively let them selves be misused; and there are, strangely enough, those who need and seek abuse.

However, do not find it strange when and where males misuse their instinctive and privileged position as leader, concomitant with injudicious domination. Such tendencies expose an abysmal ignorance of real leadership. The Lie is so insidious, only the Holy Spirit can reveal the sad, tragic, fact of doctrinal teachings ignoring the forgiveness wrought and established as reality by Jesus at Calvary for Eve. This is an outrageous insult to the sacrifice of our Lord Jesus.

Secondly: Another principle a religious church is failing to recognize is full-scale repentance (and restitution where possible.) An unrepentant church does not have clean garments, imperative if there is to be a wedding feast, and at this point in the present discourse, male intercessors should be pricking their ears. We are to beseech our Father for a mighty, holy, spirit of true repentance to sweep our church on behalf of generations of gender abuse—indescribable atrocities and injustice have been inflicted on females, irrespective of age, race or creed, or the time-table of ages.

We deny the power of God's forgiveness accomplished by the Blood shed at Calvary. Marriages will continue to disintegrate, the back of usurpation will not be broken unless we fall flat on our faces and weep into the dust for God to bring mankind to repentance and acceptance of the new life in Christ.

And one shudders at the role women play in reducing susceptible males to the level of lusting animals. It is a further disgrace when, in the ranks of Holy Spirit-inspired children of God we have, and tolerate, detected abusers sharing pews and Holy Communion. We are alerted by symptoms and warned by whisperings and still embrace them at our gatherings and fellowships without addressing their problem on a personal level. We know of them standing even in our pulpits, hammering on the sins of adultery and homosexuality. The Church suffers and her joy is a farce; her praises and worship is a stench in the nostrils of God, Who is holy and pure. Her wedding garments reek, all because of compromise and appeasement of guilty individuals.

And shall say, Cast ye up, cast ye up, prepare the way, take up the stumblingblock out of the way of my people.

For thus saith the high and lofty One that inhabiteth eternity, whose name is Holy; I dwell in the high and holy place, with him also that is of a contrite and humble spirit, to revive the spirit of the humble, and to revive the heart of the contrite ones.

For I will not contend for ever neither will I be always wroth: For the spirit should fall before me, and the souls which I have made (Is.57:14-16).

His House Divided

The tree of knowledge bore its first error when Cain was born. Then the promise to Woman of a Seed also bore fruit and Abel was born. A division had taken place in the house of Adam and Eve: Good and Evil, (opposite poles) were evidenced and no longer could the house stand firm.

We have one earth with south and north poles. And from the one womb Cain and Abel. We see the un-purged heart as shown to Ezekiel—in the same temple the Presence of both God and Satan's demons. From the heart of God came forth the letter that killeth (Mosaic Law, a curse according to the Epistle to the Galatians) and also the Living Word containing eternal life. This teaches us how opposites and extremes provide a frame of reference whereby we can measure our perceptions and information concerning any given situation or matter. Such knowledge in turn determine our persuasions, preferences, choices, decisions and even style of life, and we live our lives accordingly.

Opposites cannot ever blend perfectly, perhaps there will always be something of an imbalance and only Divine revelation can explain such thought-provoking and contradictory passages as *Joh 1:1-4, Is.45:5-8, 1 Joh.1:5-7*. Scripture throughout gives us instances of God actually speaking to people and we therefore know Him as a Person. He is not an influence, nor a force. He is Creator and the only One. He made all things. In Him we live and have our being. He dwells *in the light*, which no man can approach. Now comes Isaiah and informs us that God declares His omnipotence, also in opposites; **'I make peace and create evil.'**

There is nothing that **is** that does not come from our Father God! And still we ask: where does 'evil' come from?

The law of evil lay awaiting attention! Had Adam but taken firm stand and denied himself and his wife a taste of soul-power! One wrong, calculated choice denied them partaking of the Tree of Life and as a result the full span of millennia would keep mankind from again walking in a quickened spirit. With Cain still industriously tilling the receptive ground of our minds and sowing it with dark, murderous thoughts, and the opposite pole being the blood of Abel's sacrifice, accepted by the Most High, we may not deny the urgency of making a decision. God has given us His Son as frame of reference, but we have invitations to follow coming from either above or below, and no middle course whatsoever is set before us.

The principle of two poles operating can develop into a dualistic theology if we allow it, yet when we are come into Truth we will see how often we permit our thought life to pivot on two poles: Light and dark, good and evil. Man has a choice: he could become a god in this world, or he could in this world become free, reigning, quickened by the Holy Spirit, and ready for the return of Jesus Christ.

What will it be?

9

DEAR BROTHER PAUL

And The House United

The ripple effects of Adam's choice can never be accurately estimated. The extent of the disastrous repercussions is beyond measure, but through Christ we are already delivered from every bondage Satan can devise, therefore, a woman truly freed by Jesus has no problem with 'submission.' The men in her life need not fear usurpation of their dominion.

A woman who walks in Christ has the attitude of mind and heart that overflows in every direction and situation. A sweet yielding whether it is her husband, the older women or the leadership. It is not slavish, nor a fake. The secular world does not understand it, yet succumbs to the attraction of it. She is not even consciously exercising the quiescence and co-operation channelling such rare Holy Spirit fragrance. There is nothing disorderly or raucous about her, certainly she is not an embarrassment in any meeting, husband or no husband, as Paul obliquely suggests. She does not experience authority as a threat to her person. This woman knows pride demands submission from others, whereas genuine humility earns it. An arrogant person will not submit to another such because for him or her, a conscious effort to give in is painful, demeaning, and too much to ask—wrong thinking, misconception, and self-deception.

A humble woman has a vision; she desires this attainable goal; her aspiration is to gain 'the mind of Christ.'

She gets her priorities straightened out. She knows there is one way only of reaching her goal: *God's order—first things must always come first.* (There you are, Adam. What more would you want?) She is to submit to this specific law if she wants to achieve her goal and get the desired results.

What are 'first things' and how does 'God's order' operate?

The Apostle Paul took great pains to instil this logical, common sense principle. If you belong to Christ, then no matter who you are or what your ranking or station in life, you are to do all as if unto Christ (*Col.3:25.*) This attribute is the very first thing to start with and please believe me, there is 'order' in this approach!

Everything for man begins with a thought, an idea, or desire, and getting a clear vision of the final product.

You must know what you are aiming at, what you desire to achieve, what the mission is, or the goal.

The 'first thing' is that with which you start when working toward your specific goal.

This 'first thing' is in fact the foundation on which you will build toward obtaining your goal, which in the case of a believer is not only life in Christ, but Jesus in Person.

With the foundation thus laid, there follows the building and working toward—how you use your equipment and opportunities will determine the quality of the final product.

The goal does not fall into your lap without sacrifice and serious effort. For this reason we have been given instructions in the written Word, and the Holy Spirit as plumb line. (*1 Cor.2:15,16, Phil.2:5, and 1 Pet.4:1,2*).

Submission is the foundation for a life of excellence in Jesus, and the mind of Christ brings us fully into the will of God.

Now let us waive for a while the general earth-minded demand for submissive wives, not only the popular tenet, but also our personal concept of this knotty issue, and reappraise the word *submission.*

A *sub*-role always *qualifies* and enhances the main objective. *Qualify* is to make competent, or eligible, to make fit for a position or purpose, to equip, get ready, prepare, to condition. This understanding elevates Eve's role in marriage, and immediately we ask: what is Adam's main objective?

Emphasis is placed on possessing 'leadership qualities' yet few have first-hand, substantial knowledge of what it takes to be a leader.

A real, or good leader knows he is under obligation to submit himself to the rank, job, or mission to which he is assigned. He knows he must get himself started on the right foundation and put first things first, and then get all the secondary to follow in good order.

He does not subdue what will equip him; get him fitted and ready, prepared, conditioned and eligible.

This leader knows he is dependent on other rankings to effectively pull his mission through to completion. He knows the law of success run on the oil of right relations—interdependency—and this law does not cater to his personal needs or claims. His assignment has absolute priority and he is in submission to that priority. He cannot afford to underestimate, debase, ignore or abuse the worth of his sub-rankings or he will not achieve the purposed results.

There is no such thing as inferior ranking—inferior quality of fruit, unpalatable yes, but not inferior ranking.

The Afrikaans translation of the word submission relating to our present discussion, carries with it a different, a misleading, and unfortunate flavour: *onderdaan, onderdanig, onderdanigheid* denotes the subjects of a monarch, the underlings of a ruler. Where the spirit of religion misapplies this word, one believing partner is *made inferior, or overcome, or worsted (2 Pet.2:19b* amplified*)* and the spirit of both loses dignity. Then the devil has neatly applied *a wicked balance and deceitful weights (Mic.6:11)* and the leadership with a tendency toward legalism has not yet recognized or dealt with this deception.

Now, it is interesting to learn that 'rule' actually indicates 'to lead, to guide' and has through centuries taken on a controlling, dictatorial connotation. We can understand why *Gen.3:16* have gotten itself such a sting. Wrong thinking, wrong concept, wrong exegesis, and wrong application.

See God's perfect order in everything, taking by way of example a few words chosen at random, and examine the word submission accordingly.

Senior education is built on the solid foundation of good grounding in the indispensanle sub-standards A and B. Is a PhD for instance, the goal?

Electricity from the main power plant runs only as far as the substation would have it go—the substation reduces the high voltage suitably to meet simple consumer needs, which is the real goal.

Likewisse, a highway cannot possibly serve outlying areas without subways smartly and neatly re-streaming traffic into a further network of roads. What purpose does the entire system serve?

Stone is cut from a hole in the quarry side, and hewn into suitable pillar and foundation blocks for construction purposes. The full potential of the quarry finds expression in the completed stone building. Thus, taken from out of the hole in the first, comes forth the second, in order to accomplish the real purpose and goal of the first. In this, we recognize Adam and Eve—she coming forth from a hole in his side. We see Abraham and Sarah, taking careful note of *Is.51:1,2*. We see the Bride of Christ drawn from the hole in the side of Jesus as He hung on the Cross, her righteousness ever flowing forth from His submission to the Father's will. And now we can understand our Father's insistence on submission and sacrificial obedience.

We have been granted a profound and powerful principle in 'submission' and have gotten hold of the wrong end of the stick ...

In every instance we must ask: what is the purpose, the ultimate goal?

Would it not perhaps be wise if Adam first asked himself seriously if the Eve he proposes taking as wife, can sub his mission?

But then, should Adam not first ask himself if he knows what his mission is?

The pulpit dare not preach superficial ideas of God's order, to serve misconceptions promoted by Satan, who desires to feed a war between the sexes. Look at sub-mission from God's perspective and not from that of man; and see how the side-post on which the door hinges, is as important as the door itself, for both serve the same purpose.

Eve's ingredients provide Adam the dough, and his personal submission to Jesus bakes it to perfection for the wedding feast of the Bridegroom.

Paul was enjoining wives to come into God's order. He was imploring them to start right at the beginning, the foundation, putting first things first. He was advising them to submit their natural propensities to the Lord and thereby pour their full value into their husbands so his mission and their joint obligation to the Father could be completed in Christ Jesus.

It does not matter what the world makes of submission, submissiveness, subordination, subjugation and every other miserable distortion of leadership that has been debasing so many lives, for God is the final, supreme judge, and in the final analysis He alone grades the quality of an individual's submission.

When God brings a Spirit-quickened bride to her reborn groom, the Lord expects her to accept her new husband as the one who will direct through her very life his personal mission, his Life-giving business. And the husband who comprehends this profoundness will gain a depth and added stature to his God-inspired authority and leadership that he never dreamed possible or attainable. Of course, as administrator it depends entirely on what he does with her proffered potential.

Selfish pride thrives on submissiveness and misuses it. Submission, correctly understood and applied, changes lives and marriages. It takes two to tangle—or to tango. A man cannot expect nor demand that his wife be in submission to him if he himself is not submitted to God; he will first need to get his own ideas and ways to 'rank under' what his Father wants of him. In this Jesus exemplified. He put Himself under what the Father wanted, even up to the point of crucifixion.

In marriage, a delicate area is a husband's expression of sexual intercourse and he can make or break his image and likeness to the Father. It does not count if one is married or not, we should not even toy with the idea of phallic dominance as our inherent male rights, and instinct is no excuse for sexual abuse. Of late, and in my eightieth year, I am hearing of husbands raping their wives! What next!

Satan's hatred of Woman is manifested when females are abused, for he is ever aware of the Seed she carried that worked his defeat.

We all thrive on appreciation and recognition, and bloom on gentleness and consideration, and simply lap up approval of our person and achievements—but subconsciously we see in this petting a reflection of our own glory, (whatever tarnished glory we may have) whereas the glory should be all His. Growing into His image and likeness will therefore cost us each a lot of discipline in denying the Old Man, and we must reckon the price well worth it. God delighted in the spirit of His first children and He wanted them to be with Him in everything. He desires reciprocating love; He created us to be an expression, an extension of Himself and the hallowed purpose in creating Woman, (who was brought into this Divine love *affaire*) was to amplify the godly qualities of mankind. But the mission was, and still is, an empowered union reflecting the glory of our Heavenly Creator—the delight of His eternal heart is spiritual offspring He can call His own. We must stand in awe and also in abject misery as we repent of shallow exegesis.

Parcelled And Posted

Call her Mrs. Joan Smith. (You may also call me Mrs. Joan Smith. There are many of us about.) She had been entangled in an emotionally abusive marriage, and was still fighting for recovery when a Jewish friend invited her to attend a meeting in the local Synagogue. Joan, having previously viewed video material on one such meeting, declined. She reluctantly, if not frankly, shared her thoughts and emotions with her surprised and rather disconcerted friend, who, fortunately being a mature and sound woman, took no offence. Over to Mrs. Joan Smith:

'While watching the video, it became increasingly evident to me that Jewish tradition and customs have been transmitted from generation to generation. A known fact, is it not? I could not help but notice that the youngsters attending the procedures appeared as resolved as the male adults.

As with one voice a group of Jewish gentlemen greeted a second group, who responded to the first group with equally ardent Amens. All of this was done heartily and in the vernacular, with much movement and earnest intent. You Jews certainly are serious with God!

'Blessed art Thou, our Lord God, King of the universe, Who has not made me a heathen!' 'AMEN!'

'Blessed art Thou, our Lord God, King of the universe '*Baruch atah Adonai Eloheinu* Who has not made me a *neegre*' (a bondsman, a slave) 'AMEN!'

'Blessed art Thou, our Lord God, King of the universe, Who has not made me a woman!' 'AMEN!'

Joan: 'Is this not Ish wielding misguided supremacy?'

Friend Lea: 'I should say, yes. Yet Ish fosters good reasons, and he feels good about his reasoning. One can understand it if to a gentile (outsider) and on top of it an emotionally battered woman, all of this amounts to males superciliously allotting females an inferior position, ranking them with heathen and slaves, and thanking God for their own safe perches! We Jewish women are born to accept this'

Joan: 'I am a new Christian and getting to learn about parables, but I couldn't help thinking of the Pharisee and the publican, with the Pharisee thanking God that he cannot be ranked on par with the publican. This is my conclusion, Lea. Ish has parcelled, labelled, and posted his gift from God. And the postal address is: Limitation,
      State of Subjugation,
        The World.

Would you mind hearing me out? Women played into it. This is not only how I feel, but what I perceive, even if it is a little late in the day for me to adjust my approaches and apply newly gained insights and wisdom. Yes, I did play into it because I did not know my true worth in God. I accepted abuse and retaliated in the wrong way, yet I loved him enough to stick it out for as long as I did. I am not the first one, not the only one and won't be the last.

I am not bitter; I am simply stating facts. You see, Lea, now I know I contributed largely toward creating a dysfunctional family and a discomfiting environment because I was a victim of my own hang-ups. I was entrapped not only by ignorance but also a fear of being left destitute, and all because of my inability to honour my real self and stand squarely on my own feet. I did not know I had Godly self-worth and valid authority in Christ to expect, demand, and receive better treatment. I should have taken hold of that authority and held an unwavering, righteous stand right from the beginning. I know my contribution to our marriage should instead have been firm and of another quality. I am convinced things would have turned out differently.

Now I can look at other women objectively and I see how Isha is awakening all over the world. She finds herself boxed in. She finds she has no say in the whole matter of gender bias and is fisting the carton. She wants out.

She is leaping for the saddle, Lea, and may find herself flying right over the back of the horse, and land in the open, waiting arms of satanic rebellion. From the one extreme, to the other.'

Mrs. Joan Smith is right. The international conference for women held in Beijing some years ago was but the initial rumblings of Volcano Suppressed Woman. If she swallows another Lie, she will again be out of the will of God and find herself worse off. Satan would have caught her for a sucker yet once again. He is a hard taskmaster and not satisfied with anything less than souls burning in hell. Any form of rebellion is for the committed Christian a start on the road downhill. One is to analyse reactions and resentments, because passivity and rebellion, being the two poles, cannot ever work together and produce acceptable results.

The paradox is that Jesus brings one into conflict with customs, prejudices, traditions and areas of our thinking where we least expected entrapment. How grudgingly we relinquish ingrained assumptions to our Lord's ascendancy! How little we know of entering His rest and letting Him do our things His way!

Cooped In The Chicken Run

There is hardly a man walking this earth whose being is not influenced by his cultural background. And the Apostle Paul no less—but here we must tread carefully, for discernment is vital.

The Pauline epistles have had vast repercussions over hundreds of years. What Paul wrote on the subject of women has been applied literally, affording the Spirit of Religion sufficient ground to coop Christian women neatly in the chicken run. To even question this issue is regarded as unscriptural and is therefore summarily rejected as being out of the will of God. The mindset is a cemented one.

In considering some of the aspects of Paul's writings, one has always to **bear in mind the general status of women in Paul's time.** Although Paul strongly emphasizes the need to know the essence of his Gospel, (the Indwelling Christ *Gal.1:11,12),* he yet displays a strong streak of Judaism in dealing with women.

According to the culture of his day, they were not even addressed. LAW was being upheld. The point made here is that the Jewish mindset was confronted with the radical teachings of Jesus, and Paul preached to early Judaist churches.

Paul would by present standards be highly esteemed as an outstanding psychologist. He is believed to have been a master at his profession and probably was a brilliant advocate; but we do not fully appreciate the extent to which he was engaged in remarkably subtle spiritual warfare.

One is inclined to conclude that Paul contradicted himself on various points, but no, he was clever and his strategy superb. Wherever he went, ministered, preached, or whatever he wrote, he was deliberately 'keeping women in their proper place' and hoping thereby to gain a few male minds to concentrated, agreeable attention. **He was practicing what he was preaching**:

And unto the Jews I became as a Jew, that I might gain the Jews; to them that are under the law, as under the law, that I might gain them that are under the law.

To them that are without law, as without law, (being not without law to God but under the law to Christ,) that I might gain them that are without law.

To the weak became I as weak, that I might gain the weak: I am made all things to all men, that I might by all means save some (1 Cor.9:20-22)..

For Christ is the end of the law for righteousness to every one that believeth (Rom.10:4).

Led by the Holy Spirit, Paul enters Truth when he brings an injunctive word to the Ephesians. We have no alternative but push aside all self-opinionated assertiveness, together with this very same friend Paul's personal point of view. (Which, we are no longer reluctant to admit, he sparsely adds like a good touch of salt).

So! Why not rather appreciate and enjoy 'Paul's Love Song' *(Eph.5:20-33)* as an exceptional expression of the Lord's longing for a perfected Bride? Because, in writing these verses, he flawlessly equals the sublime love Song of Solomon for the beautiful Shulamite. The fragrance caught in both compositions, the precious mutual wooing that depicts the desire of the Lord Jesus Christ for the spirit of His beloved saints, is incomparably expressed in both writings.

Rebellious women dislike *Eph.5:22-33*. It rattles them no end and with reason, because ever since Paul wrote this letter it has been misapplied by the spirit of male superiority.

Paul's pronouncements on women reflect the conditions of his day and to us in our day he seems more than a bit unfair, but he had sound reasons for writing to the various churches as he did. Meetings in those early days of the church may be described as chaotic and some form of order had to be established. The freedom we have through the Holy Spirit when He is the Leader in any meeting is a beautiful, joyous, spontaneous and serious responsibility, and can never be fully appreciated by those who have not yet tasted of this wine.

Every letter Paul wrote covered the particular problem of the specific church and yet has bearing on all the other churches. And so Dear Brother Paul, believe it or not, resorts to 'the Law' to carry his point:

Let your women keep silence in the churches; for it is not permitted unto them to speak; but they are commanded to be under obedience as also saith the law (1 Cor.14:34).

For as many as are of the works of the law are under the curse; for it is written, Cursed is every one that continueth not in all things which are unwritten in the book of the law to do them

*But that no man is justified by the law in the sight of God, it is evident: for, **the just shall live by faith (Gal.3:10,11).***

Why should Paul find it necessary to subdue reborn, Blood-washed women, with 'the Law' in a New Testament church? What 'Law'? The Amplified suggest this verse connects with *Gen.3:16* as being the grounds for Hebrew laws on women.

Who is it laid down the rule that women are not permitted to speak, much less teach? The same 'Law'? *Gen.3:16?* Was it self-considering patriarchs who connived folklore, implemented and documented it as 'a law unto women' and therefore decreed by God? We must look to our Lord and Master and see how He handled this state of affairs.

Men are power-orientated. And this is the big bluff that took Eve captive and holds fallen Adam in bondage to Male Superiority, rarely a one after him coming into the fullness of the stature God had originally intended for him.

We have serious adjustments to make to our thinking: **Gen.3:16 is not a fundamental law**. This one verse contains only punishment: Eve's sin and punishment has been redeemed by the Blood of Jesus at Calvary and is no longer remembered, or held against Eve by our Heavenly Father.

*And, having made peace through the blood of his cross, by him to **reconcile all** things unto himself; by him, I say, whether they be things in earth, or things in heaven (Col.1:20).*

Men who still hold women in bondage, in subjection, or demand her submission on the grounds of 'the Law' are working against the redemptive and reconciliatory work of Jesus. This is serious. The Church should take firm stand and be careful about interpretation, preaching and practical implementation, for woman is no longer disabled.

There is therefore now no condemnation to them that are in Christ Jesus. The whole creation was put in the Lord when He willingly drank the cup. The whole creation was rent when His body was broken on the Cross. All of the old creation died when He died. Thus all things became new when He was risen: *'Go, tell My brethren'* and He deliberately chose a woman to be the first to 'go tell'.

Having abolished in his flesh the enmity, **even the law of commandments**, *contained in ordinances, for to make in himself of twain one new man, so making peace (Eph.2:15).*

Notice Paul on occasion giving his own mind. His personal point of view is expressed as often as he uses the first person singular 'I'.

Primarily Paul was called to speak the truth about the mystery revealed to him and for which he had been set apart. He could not afford compromise: it was an awesome revelation, to be imparted to Gentiles, and which did not exclude any Jew who would accept Jesus as his Messiah.

But when it pleased God, who separated me from my mother's womb, and called me by his grace,

To reveal his Son in me, that I might preach him among the heathen; immediately I conferred not with flesh and blood: (Gal.1:15,16)..

Paul had to go carefully. He knew how deeply ingrained cultural resistance would be against any changes, particularly parity for women. Thinking of human rights in present day terms makes one smile. Sure, enjoy a second smile for *1 Cor.9:5!*

Stilling Potential Voices

Which shall it be? God's rudiments, His everlasting principles before the fall, or, the man-made rudiments of the world system after the fall interfering and mingling with the true Word, thus dissipating our walk by faith?

Jesus provided culture shock, no doubt! His disciples raised their eyebrows when he even but spoke to the Samaritan woman at the well. In *1 Tim.2 as from verse 9* we discern Paul's approach as an overflow of the elementary rules of the Hebrew system, and where this is taught and upheld in present religious situations, the yoke-fellow spirits of Legalism and Religiosity are openly at work.

If we are going to look through our modern Western spectacles at everything the Bible tells us we will hamper our spiritual growth if we not distinguish and divide the Word correctly. Sitting still, folding passive hands, skimming the surface or absorbing any teaching because we are spiritually lazy, will not edify, rectify or purify the inner man, and will not give God the honour and glory which is His by sovereign right.

Think twice and be aware of the danger of imitating a Jewish milieu with all its external laws, offerings and feasts, a trend become so fashionable these days in certain Christian circles. The New Testament enables us to see the Kingdom of God as preached by Jesus (*Sermon on the Mount, Matt.5 etc.*) before the crucifixion, and eternal grace accomplished by the Indwelling Christ in the heart of man after the crucifixion.

Jesus charged His disciples to go take the gospel of the Kingdom to the lost sheep of Israel. The Jews rejected this gospel when they crucified Jesus because of it. The Kingdom message leads us to the Crucifixion, and we may see the Cross as an accomplishing act. The New Testament does not include external laws and works that demand upholding by either Jew or Gentile.

Neither must we discard or ignore the fundamental laws of God, given through in the Old Testament, because without them we will not grasp the grace of God. This is not a thrust of dispensation-ism—the concern is for Eve.

It is difficult for us to appreciate the pioneering done by rejected, persecuted, maligned and suffering Christian women who had been delivered by Jesus and who, in the face of torture and deprivation, witnessed and preached their Jesus and their salvation, their restoration and their release, to an angry and vengeful world!

Seriously committed Christian women are made of stuff we know not of—unless we drink of the same cup down to the dregs—when only shall we see and experience it is not our power or strength that doeth the works. Together with men, these martyrs suffered, preached, prophesied, and started house churches. The men accepted them as co-workers, equal in the Lord. They suffered torture on an equal basis, no distinctions being made between the sexes when the screws were turned on, regarded equal in strength to carry their cross and walk His Way, yet this did not eliminate an intrinsic bias!

Do not find it strange that when Paul speaks or writes to the churches, he addresses the brethren only. (How strange also legalists have subsequently not put this into practice at Christian church meetings). Paul never begins with 'Dear brothers and sisters'.

A further point of interest: Paul notes and names only brethren as having first seen and spoken to the newly risen Jesus *(1 Cor.15:4-8),* in letters written approximately 53–55 years after the crucifixion. But the accounts of Matthew in Ch.28 (written between 60–63 AD), Mark 16 (60–65 AD), Luke 24 (65–70 AD) and John 2) (85–90 AD) name the women individually and give detailed account of the glorious moment of meeting with the Risen Christ when He had just come forth from the tomb.

Could it be possible that their close association with Jesus before His death would earn them at least some credibility with the other disciples? No! *Mark*

16:11,14 also Luke 24:10,11 gives a very clear picture of the low esteem in which women were held; what they had just experienced was held of no account. Simply, they were not believed.

Of the four Gospels, John reveals the more spiritual depth and insight into the divinity of Jesus Christ and His mission. The Gospel as recorded by John is distinctly on another level as that of Matthew, Mark and Luke. John is the only one to give an indication of the Lord's very special awareness and consideration—Jesus chose Mary Magdalene—**a woman was sent with the first message to the world of the risen Son of God!**

There is far more to *Gen.3:16* than the superficial reader can appreciate and Paul's concern for the welfare of the churches can be understood. It is a terrible thing in any fellowship when Jezebel rears its head and strikes, especially so if evil control is subversively attempted or effected through a woman.

However, this threatening, devious spirit is not the subject at present under discussion. What we are dealing with now is the satanic captivity of Eve and for Satan it is of the utmost importance that her spiritual influence be either suppressed, diverted or corrupted, and keeping a slanted *Gen.3:16* alive and flourishing in the minds of both sexes is an effective strategy.

Because believers do not get a strong grip on the 'it-is-done' work of the Cross, the Church is repressed. *Tetelestai—in His death my sins are forgiven,* likewise, when I, he, her, die to self and accept Jesus, our sins are forgiven *(John 20:21-23).* When we dance to the tune Satan plays, we create a gap in our hedge.—*God sent forth His Son, made of a woman, made under the Law, to redeem them that were under the Law (Gal.4:3-7).*

Note Paul's personal injunction: *But I suffer not a woman to teach, nor to usurp authority over the man, but to be in silence (1 Tim.2:12).* Would our loving Father of all grace and mercy say to any precious male soul: 'Listen man, you have accepted My Son as your personal Salvation through teaching you have taken to heart. Good. But sorry, you may not enter My eternal Kingdom for you see, I used a woman to explain and tell you.'

Jesus was practical. He desired the Gospel of the Kingdom to reach the ears of Jews and His invitation made the gentiles as welcome as it did the house of Israel. The Gospel and teaching are inseparable. The one cannot be without the other. *Romans10* has the committed believer concerned about the harm done to seeking souls through false teaching. The subjugation of saintly women who are potential voices for God to teach Truth to those who would hear, within the church and those without who are hungering for salvation, is an effective strategy of the enemy, a very obvious ploy that is robbing the Gospel, the Church, and the world.

No one dare deny such voices to impart what the Holy Spirit has inspired. Experience has taught that when God raises Himself a voice there is an unmistakable timbre of love and undeniable authority resounding in its notes. The voice will carry a potent message of such deep persuasive holiness that all pride and prejudice will evaporate like mist in the sun, leaving the most critical, hardened heart, the most abject piece of miserable humanity, the hurt and wounded touched and stirred in their depths, and healed.

For Adam was first formed, then Eve (1 Tim.2:13). The issue here seems to be authority and rank. Undeniably, authority is very much a quality, and the calibre of being carrying it effectively, is not necessarily locked in a male frame only. The spiritual man or woman will look beyond the physical and adjust obedience according to the demands God makes on him or her in any given situation. Adam, simply because he was formed first, holds no problem for godly Eve—she smiles at the misuse of this verse.

And Adam was not deceived, but the woman being deceived was in the transgression (1 Tim.2:14). Adam was not deceived yet took and ate in spite of knowing full well that he was commanded not to eat! Deception through women and disobedience in men work hand in hand—the one not more and the other no less.

Notwithstanding she shall be saved in childbearing, if they continue in faith and charity and holiness with sobriety (1 Tim.2:15). What is it the Holy Spirit wants to explain? The use of 'she' and 'they' confuses us as to who exactly will be saved by a continued walk in faith, charity and holiness with sobriety, and the different translations are debatable. (Not everyone has access to the original texts in Greek and Hebrew).

Bringing children into this world does not save women and neither does her salvation depend on the choices her children make, or their walk in life. The lay desires further insight into verses 14 and 15, and we seek references in Scripture to explain to us what appears to be obscure. Jew or Gentile, whoever you are and whatever you may have arrived at spiritually, there is none other than Jesus Christ, Lord and Saviour, the only begotten Son of God Who is the Word, the Vine, the Truth and the Way. There is no other way through whom, or by which, salvation can be effected.

Recent publications emphasize evidence that the letters to Timothy were written at a very much later date than surmised, something like fifty years. We may be attributing to Paul the exclusion of women from offices of authority and leadership in the church, such offices first instituted only after Paul's time! Sentences have possibly been inserted and may not have come from Paul himself. The last verses of *1 Tim.2* shows a notable and disquieting contrast with the profundity of his teachings on the Indwelling Christ. Many questions without convincing or proven answers have surfaced over time and one would do well first to investigate so-called evidence. Paul very wisely advised Timothy to shut his mind against non-productive contention.

The concern is that unregenerate Christians, captivated by biased exegesis, uses it as a rod to subdue God's most beautiful creature—woman. The rape of Woman is total.

10

FREE

Personal Discipline

Significant it is how Paul's every admonishment deals with 'your own husband'. Not men, not any other man, but your own husband.

Sister, be not in bondage to traditional, contextual Hebrew laws on women, Old or New Testament. We are free to love and serve our own husbands with reverence when we yield to his healthy leading, reborn or not. If he does not, or cannot teach, then you teach when the Holy Spirit prompts you! We are not to be concerned if other men take offence. If I know myself to be a sincere disciple of Jesus, then I also know He never taught me teaching and 'discipling people' are restricted to males only. The Gospel will fight its way through every resistance.

If your own husband is not present in any church meeting, (or in other situations), then you are not subject to any other man, even if he is the leader, for one only is your 'covering' and He is your Lord Jesus. Disregard for appointed authorities, also if elected according to the system of any (religious) institution, is not part of the considerations here, so please do not deliberately misunderstand. Members of the leadership are honoured for the cloak of responsible service they wear—often not to be envied—and the protection they extend, especially against deception.

An anointed leader is aware of his dependence on the Holy Spirit, and he knows the deep urge within himself to take charge and lead the flock entrusted to his care is not something of his own making—authoritarian assertiveness will never raise its head to oust a move of the Holy Spirit working in the right climate through a woman where he is shepherding.

Such a man serves his love to others: his whole life is flooded and spilling over in tactful, firm leading. It evokes compliance and co-operation from the flock. He does not need to strive in self-effort to vindicate the position in which God has placed him; it simply flows forth in a state of being. He does not fear members will usurp his position, for they will have neither reason nor desire to do so.

Women are exhorted to come back—return, return, return to God's original purposes and intentions. Become God's woman! Comply when you have received a word of teaching. The Holy Spirit will not have you suppress it. God is not a respecter of persons. You may not refrain from giving utterance to what He is saying just because you are a woman and consider yourself unsuitable, or of no esteem.

If what you are schooling is not of God, the body as a whole will get clear warning through the Holy Spirit. They should then correct you in love, provided they have full understanding of God's Word on the subject. Female disciples are sometimes hammered with 'not being in God's order' at the high cost of losing sensitivity to the Holy Spirit's leading.

Both leadership and the body, closely knit and committed, is your protection and will keep you from error should your husband be spiritually incapable of doing so. If the Indwelling Christ is in charge you will not find it difficult to submit to leadership and accept correction from the elders should it be necessary.

If you are opposed and your spirit knows what you are saying is from God, then do not argue. Swallow the feeling of unresolved business and hold your peace; guard your utterances. Wait on the Lord to make His moves. Rest in His ability to handle His own affairs. The moment we stop fussing and flapping about something, God starts moving in. The span of time belongs to Him—immediately, a day or two, months, even years. The results and the timing are entirely His, and not to be questioned. Don't leave your study of the 'sabbath rest of God (Heb.4) at an intellectual level. Enter the rest by application. Let it become your walk, your expectation, and your personal experience by revelation. It is His power that worketh—why do we persist in feeding other influences?

People are wary of prophetesses and women teaching the Word. They cannot be blamed for this attitude because for many centuries a 'disabling law unto woman' has been a major obstacle. Appalling conduct in some quarters has also contributed. False doctrine and erroneous teaching have come through women, and their names join the ranks of well-known shepherds leading the flock astray. Unfortunately, we will always have such pressing in.

The circles in which these false teachers and leaders move are not strong enough, or sufficiently sound spiritually, to detect error. Soul-force plays a major role in spinning webs of heresy and countless people become enmeshed. Tragic if a seared conscience is the outcome for the Holy Spirit will no longer woo that one into freedom.

Please permit a word to wives who consider themselves unequally yoked with loved but unsaved husbands. Well, you have a double portion of pain and you may certainly ask Father for a double portion of wisdom and longsuffering.

No doubt you are serious with Jesus or you would not have read this far. You are married to this precious warm-hearted fuzzy who evasively and obstinately clings to any convenient reason he can conjure. (The smartest sidestepping is usually done to the refrain 'I have my church and my sport and I am okay').

The answer to this problem is not as simple as it appears: the highest activity is to enter the rest of God and cease from all self-effort. And the only way to this is through prayer, and then some more prayer. Be not discouraged or dismayed by any onslaught, for the enemy makes a study of every saint and knows where you are most vulnerable. He will use fellow saints as easily as anything else. Protect yourself with the Word and avoid commonplace statements that have no effective power-punch. Never be caught in senseless contention. Keep your walk holy and pure, do this by taking the greatest of care in dealing with the smallest detail of every moment and movement according to the Light dwelling within you.

God calls us to be spotless in our walk, waiting and ready for the Bridegroom Who is about to come. Come He certainly will, and when least expected.

PART THREE

SARAH

... and she called him lord
(1 Pet.3:61)

1

TRAPPED BY TRADITION

One Vital Link

A glimpse of the main thrust of New Testament theology is given in Leviticus and Numbers. We may never cast the Old Testament aside and ignore the riches it enfolds and the truth it reveals.

Lev.16 explains the purpose of the bullock as sin offering. Every sin I have possibly committed in my entire life is borne by Jesus Christ. In this I may understand that the Holy Spirit convicts me only of the sins I have already committed. My cleansing therefore is conditional—it is based on what our High Priest has done.

Now, my obedience to what God expects of me, including all my future choices, lies with me alone. And the very next moment already is the future! It holds all that I have not yet done!

Numbers 19 suggests there should never ever have been any yoke on any one of God's children. As it is, sin abounds and should be dealt with—the redemptive sacrifice of Jesus is effective should we find ourselves contaminated by sin or *yoked to it in some way or another*

Thus the red heifer of *Num.19* covers the sins I have not yet committed. She is offered to meet my future needs. She is a Sarah, in effect the red heifer without spot, blemish or yoke ever, killed outside the camp and reduced by fire to ashes, stood for a perfect sacrifice yet to come. He has come! He came through the link forged by Sarah's obedience, her influence, and her preservation of spiritual Isaac. As spiritual children of Abraham and Sarah, we have been supplied with sufficient for all our needs, all our lives long. We have a past, present and future supply of grace.

Is.51:1,2 clinches the position of, and the part played by this Hebrew couple in the personal spiritual history of every genuine child of God. Prophet Isaiah convincingly establishes Abraham and Sarah as the one hole, (the well, pit, quarry) from which these true ones have emerged.

How, and why, have this man and this woman earned themselves such widespread recognition?

So we return to *Gen.3:14,15,* and the first indication of the enmity between the serpent's seed and the Seed of the woman. Percentage wise, few men toy with snakes. Venomous or harmless, man finds all reptiles repulsive—this is the heritage for both man and serpent.

There is an unmistakable similarity between the devil and the snake. Cold-bloodedness is synonymous with what has no mercy or feelings.

It slithers in places, craftily hidden and unseen, lying in wait. It rears and strikes most often when least expected. It spits to blind the eyes. Nothing escapes cognisance within the radius of its darting tongue. Its fangs hook deep to inject venom containing the certainty of death. It entrances with unblinking beady black eyes, holding its prey incapacitated with fear, helpless, paralysed. It hisses to express its unmistakable intentions, human ears hearing too late. You will hear its whispering in the quiet, rather belatedly by the individual within the bustling, raucous crowd. Its embracing coils squeeze and suffocate to death. It swallows its victim whole, it consumes its own kind.

And it fears man.

Sarai may have pondered on the spiritual import of such matters as Adam and Eve, the forbidden fruit and the serpent. Noah and his family may have carried with them into the Ark a hand-me-down account of what had happened in the Garden of Eden long before Sarai's time.

Already the subjugation and slavery of the female sex was inviolably embedded, with males holding sole rights. Women had no choice but be transacted into wifehood by the patriarch as a living pawn in a tactical game of chess for his own pickings or social status, or offered as a remedy available to ease whatever might be the itch or pain of the particular moment.

Prospects for a woman were not worth a dime; it was her good fortune if the men holding sway in her life possessed a measure of decency.

Daunting to add the number of years Abraham's forbears lived considering the preciseness with which the life span of each individual is listed in the Book of Genesis. These early people had a method of reading the constellations and thereby ascertaining with correctness each year passing by and this confirms the possibility of Sarai and her peers, living in skin tents and traversing the wilderness ad lib, of knowing and doing far more intelligently and inventively than ascribed to them.

However, there is no way in which Sarai could have connected herself or her husband with the tragedy of Adam and Eve. No one predicted the radical results

her persuasive voice would bring to bear on the course of history. It was not possible for Sarai to have guessed even wildly, that both physically and spiritually,
she would be a vital link in the chain God was forging.

Sarai's conduct as recorded in the Bible verifies her lack of basic discretion and
wisdom over a long period of thwarted drive. She would be playing the same role
as Eve with a repeat performance by the same serpent with the same end in view.
The same serpent is still at work today, employing the same methods. He has no
mercy and is bent on total destruction of everyone and everything pertaining to
Jesus Christ.

Great Ones And Plain Ones

And neither could unregenerate Sarai have known the spiritual impact a reborn
Sarah would have on the sands which is upon the sea shore *(Gen.22:17)*. In His
wisdom, God carefully chooses and separates those whom He will shape and use
to further a particular purpose.

Another such chosen person was Abram. The number of old texts and the
many different translations focusing on him does bear weight, but for the time
being these are not essential to this study.

How does the casual or novice reader of the Bible experience Abraham when
reading Genesis, perhaps for the first time? Is it possible for such a person to perceive, relate and receive? Yes. With the Holy Spirit at work, comparisons can be
painfully odious, yet gloriously effective! Let us examine some of Abraham's com-
ings, goings and doings informative of the spiritual shaping that took place in the
life of a man of whom it is said he walked before God—Abraham—then see and
measure ourselves accordingly.

Time left for the Church to be making amends is short. Fresh input the Holy
Spirit supplies should be invigorated and from this platform give momentum to
full obedience in the Secret Place of the Most High.

But how, and why?

Suffice it say, Abram meticulously and audaciously built altars and openly
brought his offerings to the Almighty One, YHWH, slap inside pagan territory
practicing its barbaric and atrocious whoredoms. This does remind one of public
worship and public church life—but the actual state of affairs behind those closed
front doors? (Ezekiel makes mince of all this in his boldness of speech and conduct).

Pleasing to think of the 'great ones' as ordinary folk. When God first spoke to
Abram at Haran, he probably had every human hormone and inclination work-

ing overtime. He had reason to say to himself: 'Just think, Abe old man! You have prospects; you are still in business as much as ever before! Your God has earmarked you to be the father of many! You sure won't be forgotten!' Which is exactly how an ordinary person would think, feel, and react. This is not irreverence; bearing in mind Abram had not yet become Abraham. He was at that stage of his spiritual development in the same place as every other unregenerate Christian, audaciously helping to build another stone church slap inside modern paganism and openly bringing his tithe offerings. God Almighty is so patient with us!

Now the Lord had said unto Abram, Get thee out of thy country, and from thy kindred, and from thy father's house, unto a land that I will show thee:

And I will make of thee a great nation, and I will bless thee, and make thy name great, and thou shalt be a blessing.

And I will bless them that bless thee, and curse him that curseth thee, and in thee shall all families of the earth be blessed (Gen.12:1-3).

These weighty verses are the meaty pith of all further happenings in God's plan for a sick and angry world. May the Holy Spirit put His spotlight on each of the components contained in these three verses depicting the Bride of the Lamb.

God employs His own methods with this wayward couple. Abram hearkened unto the voice of God and left Haran, taking with him his barren wife Sarai, and his nephew Lot, and this unfortunately, was a gap in Abram's hedge. We have our first indication of Abram not being in full obedience.

Yet Abram willingly entered unknown territory when he said 'Yes! I will go!' God does this to us, in fact, He expects us to pass this first test before taking us into the next phase of our walk—if we are willing to be used of Him.

From Haran then, Abram moves on to Sichem, to the trees of Moreh, where God not only spoke again but also appeared to him. He had qualified for this supernatural move for there was within him a deeply rooted respect for the God Whose Name may hardly even be whispered: Abram had proved himself a candidate for committed set-apart obedience.

What would come next? Here at Moreh God also said to him: *Unto thy seed will I give this land (Gen.12:7).*Abram acknowledges this Presence and Promise by building an altar—but! Pulls up his tent pegs, gathers his many belongings and moves on to 'a place between'.

Now, my delight in this Hebrew hero changes to a face without smile, for I see myself. The hero is just like any ordinary believer. An awesome thing had happened to Abram at Moreh, exceptional. Called by God. Separated for future greatness, a blessing and a promise plus a bonus from God Almighty in the same breath: his descendants would be protected from anti-Semitism although, in the light of history, this particular part of the promise as noted in *Gen.12:3* seems to have been forfeited:

However, Abram would be the father of all the nations. Having gotten thus far, having built an altar at the Great Tree of Moreh to make known his gratitude and further commitment to Yahweh, one would have liked to learn another objective lesson, and to see Abram busily at work staking his claims on the land supernaturally promised to his descendents! Oh no.

When Abram broke camp at Moreh and moved further south, he did so without God's leading.

He had settled for 'a place between' *(Gen.12:8)*. He was neither here nor there. It was not Beth-el on the west and it was not Ai on the east. The name Beth-el means 'House of God' and was later derisively referred to as the 'Place of the Misleading (deceiving) Idol' and Ai, well, Ai was a 'Hill of Ruins'.

Small wonder he felt pressed to seek the face of God, so he built himself another altar at the 'place between'. Was he in an independent frame of mind where he was hoping God would talk to him again if he performed some outer religious ritual?

The altar did not help. God does not enjoy the aroma of sacrifices in an in-between position—this is a warning not to be found lukewarm, neither hot nor cold, and be spewed from His mouth. A fiery furnace was still going to be necessary and it would be a ram caught in a bush.

Abram was in disbelief when he turned his back on such a tremendous gesture and moved on to this place of his own choosing. 'In between' does not offer the right springboard to a sense of direction. After this awesome happening one would have liked to read of Abram falling flat on his face, held spellbound in speechless gratitude and adoration. But according to *Gen.12:8,9* there came from God neither a move nor a sound. So Abram gets me up and continues his trek to the South. Oh my.

Searchers are dependent on these chapters for a literal description of the man Abram; many have no other means, except for an easily available Bible, of gaining an authentic glimpse into ancient history. But even to those reading superficially, it is as clear as daylight: Abram did not strike it lucky. Not surprising.

Further south, the land was famine-stricken. How often does this happen before the lesson is learnt of not making any moves without direct indication from the Father?

Famine means not being fed properly, distressing want, forced to go on in spite of not having, forced to use every manner and means of obtaining. In a severe famine, the only thing making sense is survival and the faces of the strongest and fittest always turn to Egypt for sustenance. And the closer to Egypt the needy get, the more prone to lies—the most dangerous of all lies are the little foxes spoiling the vineyard with apparently innocuous half-truths.

The Seed Of Craftiness

I-Me-Mine is like loamy, fertile soil, tilled by Cain and ready to receive the seed spitted by whispering hisses. What was happening to Abram, the rich, altar-building, God-fearing man, first in Scripture to be called a Hebrew, happens hourly to each of us. I-Me-Mine thrives on little half-truths.

Only, this one was not a small half-truth. It was enormous, and ominous. Once again, this amazing man proves himself to be one in the bunch. When Egypt threatens to become a dangerous mess, the instinctive, primary thought flashes: 'But what's in this for me? I'm not going to be the sucker! How can I swing things so I'm safe and sound and get the best out of it all?'

Abram and his wife, in fact his half-sister, agree on a fine plan. Call it a square deal. On closer examination the deal was not as square as any woman could hope for. Egypt wanted his wife Sarai, who was fast becoming a beautiful princess and no longer a simple pawn in a game. The battle was waging in the unseen and not on any common chessboard, for Sarai was the potential Seed-bearer in lineage and Satan could not afford a slip.

Egypt offers Abram comfortable amenities and added possessions to compensate for the availability of his wife-cum-sister Sarai.

But at what price for the conscience of any sane man who professes a walk with God? Know what? There is no recorded account of Abram expressing any doubts. Adam, Adam, Adam!

When Abram was about to enter Egypt, he had said to Sarai: 'You are very beautiful and I am sure that when the Egyptians see you they will kill me because you are my wife, and let you live. Say, I beg of you, that you are my sister, so that it may be well with me for your sake, and my life will be spared because of you.' *Gen. 12:13-17* has the same throb as modern fiction—of course the Egyptian princes saw her, and of course Sarai was taken into Pharaoh;s house—and of course he treated Abram well for her sake; he acquired sheep, oxen, he-donkeys, menservants, maidservants, she-donkeys, and camels. *And the Lord plagued Pharaoh and his house with great plagues because of Sarai, Abram's wife*

Abram was concerned with self-preservation. Short-sightedly, he lost all awareness of Divine protection and the promise God had made to bless those who blessed him, and to effect curses on those who cursed him. Instead, the beautiful person of Sarai would have to do the job and get them out of a grave situation, whether she liked it or not.

Had she not agreed? Abram simply gives the impending danger an acceptable slant: his suggested plan of action might pull him through and save all his goats. Sarai was fed with 'I beg of you', melting her into co-operating with a plan seemingly feasible and made solely for her protection.

This was walking in craftiness!

As we have received mercy, we faint not; But have renounced the hidden things of dishonesty, not walking in craftiness, nor handling the word of God deceitfully, but by manifestation of the truth commending ourselves to every man's conscience in the sight of God (2 Cor.4:1,2).

How long does it take before truth hits home? Subsequently, a heathen Pharaoh enriched this man of God with material compensation for intimate access to his wife Sarai. For God the matter was grave. The link in His chain was being defiled in Egypt. God was angry. He had set Sarai apart from other women for His divine purposes, had separated her for an enormous future task, and because of fear, self-deception, unbelief and disobedience, she was pawned by her husband into a pagan harem of living royal toys.

These two prominent men each would pay a price. How much will it take before present-day Pharaohs will connect the scourging with plagues of himself and his household with an act totally out of order? Even when committed by any member of his immediate family because of its undetected satanic origin?

There is nothing written about Abram having any compunctions—avarice had also crept in. Business is business! This is not speculation; Abram accepted the compensation offered him by Pharaoh without any show of reluctance and left, taking with him his added riches and his abused wife. Perhaps Sarai took secret delight in an ego-trip; he is, after all, the Pharaoh, you know! Or was the whole episode a shaming experience, degrading, wounding to the extreme to find herself cast into the compulsory role of cheap bedfellow to such refined coarseness as the Pharaoh epitomized, by her own husband?

2

STEEPED IN CUSTOM

Eve Serves The Purpose

Shaping never stops until God is satisfied. The right moment for perfecting His plans comes at His bidding only. He has so often to repeat lessons and tests, and, as often His children do not respond as He would have them do. Abram was again tested with the same situation and he resorted to the same selfish scheming: although King Abimelech proved to be a different kettle of fish *(Gen.20)*.

The physical beauty of his wife was presented to Abram's receptive mind as the most suitable means of preserving his life and his possessions. It worked the first time, it would work again, their marriage bed defiled, the promise made to him by God underestimated and pushed aside. Forbearing, promise-keeping God would put up once again with Abrams's untrusting nonsense. In spite of his altar building and sacrifices offered, their close walk and fellowship, Abram did not have the faith in God to keep him and his intact in the face of impending disaster. His Eve would serve the purpose.

Later, and from a religious Law-keeping Jew's standpoint, there would have been much hullabaloo if his wife were the one found to have crept into another man's bed. She would summarily have been stoned to death … serve her right … I can do it, but she can't. I can sell her out if I want to … she has no voice nor choice … she has to listen to me … I know best … she hasn't got anywhere else to go … she can't even think for herself … she has to do as I tell her … I may if I want to …

Gen.13. Abram collected his goods, went up out of Egypt, and journeyed on from the south as far as Beth-el, to the place where his tent had been pegged before and he had built an altar. Here Abram again called on the name of the Lord. He was back in square one, at the 'place between' yet we sense a difference.

The tempering of Abram is beginning to show. He had faithfully called on the Lord all the time. Apart from accumulating many riches, he is also growing in stature. At times his footsteps are marked by humbleness. God can humiliate us, but we must choose to be humble; (sentiment and emotion is something entirely different) Abram gave his nephew Lot the opportunity of choosing first between going either left or right, thereby letting Lot separate himself in peace and move on to the east, the valley of Jordan.

High Tide And Low

Abram had left a gate open at the beginning of his journeys—partial obedience. He had in the very first instance received instructions to leave all at Haran. What does Abram do? *And Abram took Sarai his wife, and Lot his brother's son, and all their substance that they had gathered, and the souls that they had gotten in Haran, and they went forth to go into the land of Canaan (Gen. 12:5).* This man had fellow-shipped with God! Just what is the matter with this man!

Abram was able to hear God speaking to him but he, like us, was inattentive and did not really *hear.* Add unbelief, doubt and disobedience and we take an unnecessary forty-year trek through the wilderness. Learning the hard way because we will not stop, listen, and forsake our hasty works of the flesh.

As with Abram, when the call comes to follow God in committed surrender, the last strands of family ties have to be broken before the Lord takes further steps with His child. It was when finally he let his nephew go his own way that the Lord spoke again to Abram, and this time he had to hear the command. There could be no sidestepping or backchat. *Arise, walk through the land, the length of it and the breadth of it, for I will give it to you (Gen. 13:17).*

He did so, building altars and serving God wherever he went. Eventually Lot desperately needed his uncle. Abram's help was immediately available. This chapter is marked by the growth of Abram, whose shores were hit by low and high tides. His meeting with King Melchizedek shows the changes taking place for he gave Melchizedek a tenth of all he had taken in spoil.

To the king of Sodom, a defeated man, he said: *I have lifted up mine hand unto the Lord, the most high God, the possessor of heaven and earth*

That I will not take from a thread even to a shoelatchet, and that I will not take any thing that is thine, lest thou shouldest say, I have made Abram rich, save only that which the young men have eaten, and the portion of the men which went with me (Gen. 14:22-24). One translation reads that Abram lifted his hand, saying: *I take nothing for myself!* High tide! Abram could see the horizon of full surrender luring him when he was on the crest of the winning wave.

It is so difficult to cast aside an opportunity of indulging the practices previously a natural part of one! Abram had found it easy to utilize every means of collecting riches, and above passage is an example of how we are called upon to surrender the inclination to exploit an enticing proposition, (often at another's expense, and not only financially).

Take Scripture at random and a perfect instance is the inter-action of Jacob and Uncle Laban *(Gen.30:31)*. Jacob certainly was not at a loss for he displayed craftiness supreme. Moreover, the chronicler gives us to understand that God was avenging the dishonesty of Laban by adding to the riches of Jacob! With a breach in the wall evil will, and does enter—offspring and other members of the immediate family all too often carry a streak of the malady. Rachel succumbed and walked into outright thieving. What a price to pay for dishonesty and craftiness! Accumulating possessions, as did Abram, was a particular trait of this ingenious clan.

However, Abram was on the crest of the wave when he saw the distant shores of the Kingdom, and his vision of future citizenship by faith never left him. It was counted to him as righteousness.

3

HELD BY HABIT

Every Speck

Genesis describes the kind of man that husbanded Sarai. We know she lived a lie at the request of her scheming spouse and at cost to herself, in order to save them and theirs.

It seems as if most of God's supernatural dealings with Abram receded into spells of haziness for he too often forgets or ignores the radical and imperative call on his life.

Why is this so? New believers should not find this strange. We thrill to His voice; those intense experiences touch and transform us progressively, yet afterward we retain only the essence of what had transpired, of what had come through in the wonderful moments of visitation.

Encounters should be sufficient to carry and support the saint in a steadfast plod through the inevitable dry patches when he begins to think God has forgotten or forsaken him. This is the time when he is in danger of relapsing into what can be described as 'surface survival'—just floating along, on the crest of the wave and then down in the trough, unable to see what he saw when on top.

Where was this exceptional man's trust in his mighty Jehovah? Why does his faith appear so erratic? Because he was so much like we are: often and understandably floating at low tide. Shallow waves, less vision, the deep trough experiences less frightening, rising up on the crest occurring less often, dwindling faith; passive floating holding far more danger—with only the inner man convinced that Jehovah had not forgotten but would again make His call.

And after these things the word of the Lord came unto Abram in a vision, saying, Fear not Abram; I am thy shield, and thy exceeding great reward.

And Abram said, Lord God, what wilt thou give me, seeing I go childless, and the steward of my house is this Eliezer of Damascus?

And Abram said, Behold, to me thou hast given no seed; and lo, one born in my house is mine heir.

And behold, the word of the Lord came unto him saying This shall not be thine heir; not he that shall come forth out of thine own bowels shall be tine heir.

And he brought him forth abroad, and said, Look now toward heaven and tell the stars. If thou be able to number them: and he said unto him, So shall thy seed be and he believed in the Lord; and he counted it to him for righteousness (Gen.15:1-16).

What an immense wave! When God has spoken to us we fall into a thick darkness and a deep sleep holding terror, and shuddering fear overcomes us, giving an indication of the awesome power of a pure and holy God. Many children of God, subsequent to Abram, can testify to exactly this experience.

Yet it seems so inconsistent that Abram, in the face of Divine prophecy and revelation, still handled his private affairs as if untouched by the hand of God.

Even so, a holy fire from above has yet to come down and consume what we offer Him. Every speck of dross must be separated, removed, and put on the kindling wood. Abram was no exception. If we thus lay ourselves upon the altar in total surrender, then the slightest twinge and whining when He strikes the match will have Him stay His hand. This is where the sheep and the goats are separated—the deeply committed and the half-hearted.

Blunt Instruments

Nothing eradicates the marks left by a supernatural encounter with God and yet we are inclined to ignore or grade down the inner knowing that war is continuously being waged in the spirit world. We forget we are components of the great Architect's structure, and how vital it is to stand firm in what God has implanted in us if we are going to be of any use to Him in these end time battles.

Abram does not show, at this stage of his life, that he fully understood the implications of his contribution to a manoeuvre of extreme importance. This man of God was not yet ready for a change of name. He had received a visitation and stupendous promises, and needed confirmation (indeed thrilling stuff recorded in *Gen.15:18-21)* **but how much of it all came through to Sarai?** For this important lady feature nowhere in the schooling of Abram—and still Abram was not yet ready to become Abraham!

God has to turn His flame on, scorching, searing, full blast in the inner man, before a change of heart is sufficiently wrought to satisfy Him. Abram would trip and fall again, often, and we take lesson and solace from the readiness of his fighting spirit to recoup. Our Father does not discard a blunt instrument. He patiently hones and whittles away as He waits to keep His promises and complete His perfect plans.

4

WHAT PRICE A SON?

Flesh Of His Flesh

Considering the subordinate position of women, we have reason to doubt that Sarai was permitted any serious part in Abram's decision-making, nor could she have had a snowball's hope of openly opposing such a powerful personage as her husband evidently was. It is not strange to find Abram, the acknowledged hero, receiving more attention from chroniclers than his wife, and one can conclude Sarai was conveniently addendum. She trots along in his wanderings—he may or may not have shared with his wife his encounters with God.

Nevertheless, there were no options for Sarai but compliance to whatever her husband chose. Subjugation is born out of tradition, custom, and habit. The over-all mind-set is deeply rooted and thus her weapons would be the same as those used by thousands of other women, thwarted women.

Here the Holy Spirit is saying something, for this is a classic example, and a firsthand piece of God's mind, plus a sharp rap over the knuckles—hear the believer in his church gathering: WE MUST DO something! WE Christians must get things going. What we SEE is so VERY obvious! WE have authority in Christ and WE MUST USE IT!

Sad misconception! If we not wait on God to initiate the moves when He has already bespoken the results then disastrous the consequences. So this is what happened: **Sarai pre-empted. And Abram did all the work.**

Do not judge her. Her world was very different to ours this day. Consequently, her reasoning and reactions would play into the scenario of her particular place in time and history. Finding herself at a distinct disadvantage, without spiritual wisdom and discernment, Sarai unwisely nurtured and promoted unhealthy thinking. She gave utterance to her reasoning, acted on her innate desires, and walked into the serpent's trap. His whispering hisses adroitly set her persuasive skills aflame—female influence.

There is a difference between hoping for, wishing for, wanting to, deciding to, my will to—and faith.

Abram has no heir. Any tremendously powerful and wealthy man who had earned himself status and standing in the political arena, or who had shrewdly built himself big business and finance, who was successfully ruling and reigning over his empire, has one big overwhelming desire: a son.

A son who would take over and carry on in his father's footsteps, doing better and accomplishing even more, who would protect the family's honour, bear his father's name, and establish descendants in that name.

If he does not have a son, to what extent and extremes will such a man go to ensure he begets a true heir? Considering the primeval, progenitor instinct of human beings, there is sympathy for men and women who have permitted this void to develop into relentless pain.

Abram was a man indeed separated. Very few men or women have had direct assurance from God that he or she would eventually, and in spite of circumstantial and physical evidence to the contrary, have a legitimate son!

Historians have held us in breathless interest and so have romantic fiction writers entertained us with love and bloody murder. With plots and scheming, subterfuge and intrigue, suicide and inheritances, titles and wayward expatriates, abdications and abductions, divorce and enforced wedlock, adultery and blackmail, gangsters and illegitimate sons suddenly cropping up to claim their rightful position, whatever! Yet history and fiction make one statement, and have one predominant cry: 'Take your blood tests! He is my son and I am his father!' The heart-cry of the son is the same: 'He is my father! All that he has, is mine and all that he is, I am!'

Lo, a voice out from heaven said, This is My Son, My Beloved in Whom I delight! (Ps.27, Is.42:11).

When Abram bemoaned his sad and needy state to the Lord God, he was answered: *but he that shall come forth out of thine own bowels shall be thine heir.* Coming out of flesh of his flesh. Sarai his wife *(Gen.17:15,16)* was the only one in the eyes of God who qualified as flesh of his flesh. The true heir could not come through any substitute however subtly implanted by the enemy. It would not be by Hagar the Egyptian bond slave, and neither could it be the Damascene servant Eliezer. For the Lord was setting the stage and raising Himself a Sarah who would cope, she who was not even halfway through her own journey in the wilderness.

And Sarai said unto Abram,Behold now, the Lord hath restrained me from bearing: I pray thee, to go in unto my maid; it may be that I may obtain children by her. **And Abram hearkened to the voice of Sarai.** *(Gen.16:2).*

Sin Conceiveth Sin

The fruit the person of Hagar represented may have appeared particularly luscious what with unregenerate Sarai's carnal impatience taking the place of God's plan and timing. The same insidious whispering hisses heard in the Garden of Eden! Sin conceiveth sin!

The serpent lay coiled and ready to strike. The trash and indecency continually impressed on eager and willing minds in this advanced day, does not differ at all with what was considered acceptable social practices in the ethics of Sarai's time. Nothing shocks and anything passes as the norm—after all, Abram was a man, was he not?

Sarai's logical plan and persuasive voice did the trick for Abram's conscience … a man is as old as he feels, and he never stops feeling … no, not such a bad idea at all … she's quite a nice piece, this girl from Egypt … no, there's nothing irregular about doing this! Everybody else does it! After all, we all have at some stage or another taken our slave girls as concubine, surely God will understand me making this bid, it is some years since He promised me many descendants and I am advancing in years, am I not? I must help God on a bit … God helps those who help themselves … really, Sarai is fast ageing … not MY fault if she's barren, the fault just couldn't be with ME, could it? Of course, it is a shameful thing to be barren. I've seen her crying. I'm pretty sure she's feeling awfully guilty for not coming up with the required goods: an heir for me, her lord. Yes, I'll help her ease her pain, and together we'll help God along … an heir! And how I love her notwithstanding! Of course, this was her idea, not mine, yes, stupid to think God won't understand! **Let's do it!**

The fangs had penetrated and the deadly venom injected. Their joint decision would rock many nations over many centuries. Poor, poor Sarai.

She was desperate. (She did not know Abram would again take a wife for he was not *that* old). The point to make and accept, and of tremendous importance, is that God had chosen Sarai and would have none else establish the lineage for the Son to come. A second wife just was not good enough; it had to be Sarai, Abram's true wife. If only Sarai could have realized this! God was not going to use the bloodline of Hagar and Ishmael, nor of Keturah, or any of her six sons by Abraham. *And Abraham gave all that he had to Isaac (Gen.25:51).*

5

SABOTAGE FOILED

The Essential Contrast

Basic human tendencies have in four thousand years odd not changed one iota. Intrinsic behavioural patterns have deep roots. When the maidservant Hagar conceived, she held contempt for her aged barren mistress; this often happens when a nothing becomes a something. Contempt versus Pride.

Man has never really changed, has he? Childless Sarai felt her top position in the hen-pecking system threatened; her perch on the ruling rung of the ladder had suddenly become wonky. Ethos would not have Sarai react any other way: her thinking fell in ruts run deep by custom and she may not even have recognized the root cause of her emotional pain.

Not many unregenerate persons can read and direct their emotions and reactions with courageous honesty, because this is entirely a work of the Holy Spirit on the conscience, and has to be recognized as Truth working toward correction, right standing with God and man, and spiritual growth. Unregenerate Sarai turned sour.

She was jealous. And vindictive. These raging forces vented spitefulness and injury. In her hot bitterness, vehemence roused courage; she adamantly stood on 'her rights' and this time a rather meek Abram conceded. Hagar, misused, pregnant, bullied and resentful, took flight into the wilderness where the timely intervention and advice of the Angel of the Lord bade her humble herself, return whence she had come, and submit to her mistress. *(Gen.16:7-10)*.

Hagar's contribution to our spiritual awareness is of tremendous importance. The role she plays has noteworthy aspects deserving of analytical attention and if we can discern the principle of submission working overtime, we have ourselves an absorbing study.

In lacking insight, and being unwilling to yield unless we first know what it is all about, we often see a situation as demanding and unfair. We put our full focus on the unfairness of having to yield against our grain, and then obstinately refuse to yield! Should we surrender to our stiff-necked rebellion, we negate a calculated manoeuvre by the Father to upset the enemy's apple cart. The Lord then patiently has to start all over again to get His planned results.

Could it be that the Angel of the Lord had given Hagar far-sighted vision into the ages to come? The obedience and return of Hagar the bond slave, the little nothing, proved to be a key factor because the Remedy for the fiasco caused by Sarai's inciting disappointment and Abram's lusty impatience could run only on the oil Hagar's humble servitude provided. The principle of two opposing poles, Light and dark, Isaac and Ishmael, were components to be used of God in a display of His powerful and loving involvement with the restoration of man. For the nation Israel, it has meant persecution, genocide, blood, pain, and for the spiritual descendants of Abraham, the true Israel, much more. Much more.

Rom.9:17-24 is important to understanding Sarah and the role Hagar plays in history.

Satan thought he had composed the perfect overture to his final victory. A major theme in the composition he was orchestrating was the disobedience of Abram and Sarai. Ishmael, a product of Egypt who would in turn also marry Egypt *(Gen.21:21)*, was neatly lined up to take the place of the true heir yet to come.

Father God had His plan to salvage the human wrecks strewn along the road to eternity, running in first gear. Being Light Himself, He always employs the essential contrast of dark to show the difference He initially would not have Man know. He used the obedience and submission of Hagar, unwitting instrument of Satan, to turn the tables on the Evil One who had again so subversively and successfully aroused dark carnal desires in man in an attempt to sabotage the incarnation of Jesus Christ. The battle, on earth and in the heavenlies was, and still is, between good and evil.

Thus Biblical history gives the sad facts of two men who had replaced the direct voice of God speaking to them with those of their counterparts *(Gen.16:2)*. Adam had hearkened unto the voice of his wife and so burdened earth with fallen man. Abram had hearkened unto the voice of his wife: impatient, hasty Abram sowed, and earth was burdened afresh. It literally received a race totally enslaved and which, according *Gal.4:24,25*, still genders to bondage. Take note of the present tense.

So we read of Hagar returning and submitting to humiliation, of Ishmael being born and making his presence felt in no uncertain terms *(Gen.16:7-16)*. And of Abram becoming father at the age of 86.

A different kettle of fish, this Ishmael. He proved himself to be what it was prophesied he would be: *And he will be a wild man; his hand will be against every man, and every man's hand against him; and he shall dwell in the presence of all his brethren (Gen. 16:12)*. Taking several translations and exegesis into account, these passages reveal portentous significance in present world events.

Ishmael is as much in bondage to his heathen state now as in Abram's tent, and as much a threat to Israel now as ever before. Islam holds sway over millions and are an ominous threat, to the Jew and to Christianity. Remember though, that as a nation Ishmael cannot partake of the Promise *(Gal. 4:28-31)*. Jesus however, invites the *individual* to accept Him as Lord and Saviour and if the individual does, the persecution will be bitter for him because Ishmael will hunt any young Isaac unto death.

No person can ever appreciate the grace of God as displayed in the Garden of Eden, unless contrasting factors force him to recognise his fallen, sinful state and confronts him with a decision. God expects us to relinquish our independence so He can again take control or our lives.

A Change Of Name

And when Abram was ninety years old and nine, the Lord appeared to Abram and said unto him, I am the Almighty God walk before me, and be thou perfect.

And Abram fell on his face; and God raised him, saying,

Neither shall thy name any more be Abram, but thy name shall be Abraham, for a father of many nations have I made thee.

And God said unto Abraham, As for Sarai thy wife, thou shall not call her name Sarai, but Sarah shall her name be.

And I will bless her, and give thee a son also of her: yea, I will bless her, and she shall be a mother of nations; kings of people shall be of her

Then Abraham fell upon his face, and laughed, and said in his heart, Shall a child be born unto him that is an hundred years old? And shall Sarah, that is ninety years old, bear?

And Abraham said unto God, O that Ishmael might live before thee! (Gen. 17:1,3,5,15-18).

In ancient times, a change of name descriptively indicated a decisive, determinant occurrence in that person's life.

Why does a man fall on his face? Twice? These must have been moments of honesty, reality, shock of truth. God spares no one when He confronts us with our hearts, minds, and very lives. Nothing remains hidden to us about ourselves in a personal clash with Deity when the Holy Spirit pulls off our masks and we see all the ugliness beneath the outer veneer. How humiliating, terrible, and at the same time exhilarating, to experience the ego being broken before God with agonizing clarity!

Rebirth brings with it horror at what we are at core. Everything is brought under His searing Light and the scalpel He applies cuts right into kidney and marrow. Nothing about ourselves, before or after, can be denied or ignored again; nothing can ever be the same. We receive a conscience refusing to be smothered, inexorably it draws us back to the Source of life, in spite of the mistakes we still make.

A man in the dust, flat on his face before Yahweh, God Almighty; Abraham's laughter could have meant any number of things. Was he astounded? His emotions could have held sheer delight! Possibly. (Gen17:17). Sarcastic laughter and unbelief in the presence of the Almighty One? Doubt? Yes. A legitimate heir begotten, conceived, born to Abraham and Sarah at such advanced years? Impossible! Impossible!

Again Abraham doubted the word of the miracle-working God he had worshipped and honoured with sacrifices upon the many altars he had built on his way through the Promised Land—and, together with his distrusting laughter came the staggering truth, the enormity of what he had really done. Oh yes, had he not always suppressed the nagging thought? Ishmael is his own son, *but* he cannot ever be a trueborn! He, Abraham, only now realized what Abram previously could not. ISHMAEL SHOULD NEVER HAVE BEEN!

Ishmael! A wild, rebellious ass, (an indication of his nomadic ways), living in enmity on the borders of all his kinsmen to the east. Again we have many interpretations to consider, but the most convincing passages concerning Ishmael and Isaac is the everlasting covenant God established with Isaac, who would be born fourteen years later than his half-brother Ishmael. In direct contrast, no covenant was made with Ishmael.

And as for Ishmael, I have heard thee: Behold, I have blessed him and will make him fruitful and will multiply him exceedingly; twelve princes shall he beget, and I will make him a great nation.

But My covenant will I establish with Isaac, which Sarah shall bear unto thee at this time in the next year.

And he left off talking with him and God went up from Abraham (Gen.. .17:20-22).

Isn't it just too typical, the way we all react when cornered—this time it isn't Adam bleating and blaming Eve. This time it is Abraham's plaintive wail echoing down the centuries. One can almost hear him: 'Oh please God, let my Ishmael live before thee!'

How we cling to our illegitimate practices, how we protect what should not be permitted in our walk with God, how we nurture and keep alive at all costs what has become to us our personal pride and joy and yet is so grievous to the Lord! How, in weak moments, we revive and treasure memories of past lustful, secret indiscretions that have, nonetheless, been washed away by the atoning Blood of Jesus! How we want the Holy Spirit to pass us by, and not remind or convict the conscience, and how we want God to bless our indulgences!

6

GETTING TO KNOW SARAH

No, My Darling Wife

As was the case with Adam and Eve, no trace in Genesis is found of God addressing Abram's wife before her transgression. The responsibility of obedience to the commands of God lay with Abram and this responsibility included his wife.

With the rebirth of Abram, having become Abraham, God embraced also his flesh of his flesh, his wife Sarai. These weighty passages give informative, supporting evidence of God's provision where there is a genuine union of man and woman, and one partner has not wholeheartedly accepted Jesus. Paul gives New Testament backing on this sensitive issue: *For the unbelieving husband is sanctified by the wife, and the unbelieving wife is sanctified by the husband: else were your children unclean, but now are they holy (1 Cor.7:14).*

It was their husbands on whom the responsibility of protective spiritual obedience was placed. All hinged on Adam and Abraham's 'walk before Me and be thou perfect' because both men had received the breath of Life: God-consciousness. Remember Adam could hear God speaking to him, giving him instructions; he had fellowshipped with Him in the cool of the day. Abraham also had a close and vital relationship with God—they both knew God. These two women, Eve and Sarai, were vulnerable and exposed to their own dangerous thinking. They were left without the protective covering cloak so supernaturally woven around families when husbands obediently place their personal submission to God first in all.

A tall order? No. It is plainly stated: *'walk before Me and be thou perfect.'* If God says it is possible, then, possible it is! God does not expect from us what He knows we cannot handle. He provides the wherewithal for His children to live up to His mark. Sarai had trespassed on the Lord God's terrain when she resorted to persuading Abram contrary to Divine revelation. Why don't you … I thought you said … things aren't working out … just get going … **do** something …

With short-sighted human reasoning this couple did not understand that God does not tolerate interference with His wisdom, timing and omnipotence. Sarai had done the planning and Abram had complied.

He could have said: 'No, my darling wife. God has made His promises and covenants, and He knows you desire children and I want a true male heir. Quieten down some more, honey, I know you worry about being barren, but let's rather reconsider and not precipitate. I know we are not getting any younger but let us hang on a bit. You are my true wife, and I love you. It's been a long time, sweetheart, and I may not have told you everything He spoke to me, but I am sure He will keep His word.'

Listen, parents! And listen, Church. If, in early youth, you have never been disciplined and taught the meaning of No! then in later years you cannot take a No. Nor can you say NO! and mean it.

Eve and Sarah represent the spiritual influence of God upon the conscience of man, but it must be nurtured, kept whole and unpolluted by man himself. Her influence is God's provision and gift to him—it should be a wellspring of pure Holy Spirit water to quench his thirst whenever he needs it. However, females have the ability to exercise either constructive or destructive influence, but more often than not they mix it. Influence is dangerously close to control. A colossal responsibility has been laid on the beautiful shoulders of Isha, but Satan took hold of it instead of Adam and Abram, and succeeding males have not fully retrieved it.

Theologians have given much attention to Abraham and his son Isaac (whom he almost sacrificed as typifying God and His Son Jesus dying on the Cross and of what it cost our Father God to go to this extreme), but it is high time cognisance and study of the consequential work of Sarah be made.

Full comprehension of 'Sarah' is imperative and vital to those couples that would dare place themselves, and their partnership, on the altar in obedience to God's call on their life together.

'Sarah' takes on staggering dimensions in the spiritual realm. I would, if I could, impale you with the cardinal importance of vitalizing any 'Sarah' in your midst.

But then you must get to know her first.

And they said unto him, Where is Sarah thy wife? And he said, Behold, in the tent.

And he said, I will certainly return unto thee according to the time of life; and, lo, Sarah thy wife shall have a son. And Sarah heard it in the tent door, which was behind him.

Now Abraham and Sarah were old and well stricken in age; and it ceased to be with Sarah after the manner of women.

Therefore Sarah laughed within herself, saying, After I am waxed old shall I have pleasure, my lord being old also? And the Lord said unto Abraham, Wherefore did Sarah laugh, saying, shall I of a surety bear a child, which am old?

Is any thing too hard for the Lord? At the time appointed I will return unto thee, according to the time of life, and Sarah shall have a son. Then Sarah denied saying, I laughed not; for she was afraid. And he said, Nay, but thou didst laugh (Gen.18:9-15).

The Language of Laughter

Abraham had had his laugh. Sarah likewise could not contain hers; secret mirth discrediting God. She eavesdropped, standing in a place where she thought no one would see or hear her. When derisive laughter and doubt crystallise, separation from the will of God develops. (Even though you, together with your husband, have only just been spiritually regenerated). As with Abraham, the quality of her laughter cannot be placed—she may have been delighted, taken up by the prospects of a baby son, but then, why deny her laughter?

Sarah's problem was despairing unbelief. Had she but known, had they both but known about the Lord's spiritual order, she could have entered the rest of God many years before and through her husband's faith and perfect walk, let the Almighty come forth with all the evidence contrary to her own diagnoses. But this quality of faith and a perfect walk was not evident. Neither of them came up to the mark until such time as God had dealt even more drastically with them.

Sarah had serious thinking to do after the visitation of the three angelic men *(Gen.18:1-19)*. No one can have an encounter of such magnitude and come off scot-free. Changes in Sarah were inevitable and not necessarily pleasant. Never has there been a birthing without labour pains. *Gen.3:16* has meaning stretching beyond limited human assessment.

Read between Sarah's lines and hear the language of her laughter: 'What, ME? A child this time next year? Unbelievable. God Himself wounding and mocking me? Can I pray a child into being? No. How long have I not prayed? No, it doesn't work. My husband and I too old … No, this is painful to the extreme … I have not been used of God before … no … He has always overlooked me. These visitors are having their fun at my expense. As if the humiliation and the suffering of being despised for my barren state have not been enough. This *hurts*.

Enough is enough. Shocking. I can't take it anymore. If people carry on like this, I'll kill myself. They can drown for all I care! Another inch or two and Ishmael will be levelling me, eye to eye. No flinching there, he is beginning to stare me down. Next, he will be shouting me down. He is a strapping lad, for sure, but already masculinity and arrogance are manipulating me into subordination. Of course, I'm only a woman, an old one. Well, I won't have it. For thirteen years Hagar has flaunted her secure position as mother of Abraham's heir and it's my fault, entirely. I should never have suggested this course of action; this bed I have made up for myself ... I must sleep on it. My own fault, not any help from Abraham. He is too taken with his son. I am not anywhere in it at all. I don't count for anything and now these men come with a prediction, a far-fetched story. As if I could rouse physical lust, what the heck! And in any case, Abraham isn't up to it either. As if God cares! Ridiculous, absolutely ridiculous.

If we can hear Sarah's wry laughter, we can hear our sarcasm surfacing to ease an embarrassing sense of having lost the game. Inadequacy goads the ego and dents the pride—Sarah was a woman conspicuous for her beauty, but it was no longer a salve to her wounds and anguish.

Anyone in like circumstances would land in a rut of self-accusation. Feelings of guilt and failure are hauled onto the bandwagon and the load becomes bigger and heavier, the ruts deeper and deeper, and cynicism, bitterness, rejection, depression, fear, and other members of the same demon grouping, also jump on for a free ride. Sarah was in despair and no one with understanding, knowledgeable and compassionate, who could help unload, lift the wagon out of the ruts, and get it going again.

But let's see how Sarah handled herself—after the visitation.

Would she reload her wagon with the same old rubbish? She did not.

Sarah stood alone. She appears to have been without support and this in itself is severe schooling. With her pain swaddled in sarcasm and her self-image demolished, she was being prepared; her suffering essential for the task that lay ahead. The Divine encounter provided the needed shock and the changes would soon be evident.

By now you would have noticed that Genesis revolves around God's interaction with male characters filling the important roles. The chronicler is protecting the image of Abraham as man of God and prophet, and he gives little or no dues to any female act, which is nothing but, putting it mildly, functional to recorded history. This aspect of Genesis has not as yet received second thoughts, even if it is there for all to see. Perhaps the author comes through as a sour feminist, but would you not rather reconsider your conclusions concerning the first book of the Bible? The Holy Spirit is certain to reveal much more to the perceptive searcher, because Sarah is full of hidden surprises

7

WALK BEFORE ME

Divine Intervention

Abraham was commanded to walk perfectly before God, but fell far short He was a cheat and a liar. He was a conniving schemer, an opportunist. He was insensitive and selfish. He was not only a coward at heart, but also a physical one. Abraham practiced double standards.

Yet—Sarah called him lord *(Gen.18:12, 1 Pet.3:6).*

In stirring contrast to Abraham, the character of Boaz immediately recognises in Ruth the qualities prerequisite for an intimate walk with God and himself in marriage.

Boaz does not delay in making up his mind about Ruth. He provides, protects, and exerts his gentle and undeniable authority. He does not hesitate to express his appreciation of her character. He sustains and supports her and takes firm stand in public on her behalf. He lets the world know what he has found in precious Ruth. He cherishes her—*And Boaz spread over her his wing.*

But then, you see, Ruth had **uncovered the feet of Boaz and there she lay herself down** *(Ruth 3:7).* Profound.

What strange qualities did Sarah emanate at 89? So inciting Abimilech that he took her into his harem? Surely, the fascination she held for the King of Gerar could not be physical only?

The younger folk talk about 'chemistry' and the possibility is acceptable; something like that does exist between the sexes but surely! at Sarah's ripe old age? How old could Abimelech have been?

Constraining our smiles, we must agree something was happening for Sarah after the encounter with the Angel of the Lord *(Gen18:15).* Her spirit, soul and body were in a process of renewal. King Abimelech was a heathen but no simple country bumpkin, and he will probably tell us he could not put his finger on the attraction. Was it an aura of spirituality radiating from her person?

If so, then unlikely she was aware thereof. An air of *separated-ness* does hang over people who have had a deep cleansing experience and unconsciously others are drawn to them. This makes of Abraham a contradictory figure although leniency should be extended. With some the changes and shaping are quick and keen (Apostle Paul), with others the spiritual development after birthing, takes place at a steady pace over many years and is deep though not as spectacular.

The changes wrought goes on until the last breath and there is no one exempt from blunders; Abraham was bound to slip! I-Me-Mine does not relinquish its grip so easily and Abraham was no exception, even if his encounters with the Most High God, stretching over many years and with intermittent dry periods, was extraordinarily dramatic and awesome.

To Say The Least, Despicable

Sarah, advanced in years and obviously a well-preserved woman, was aware of her sexual condition. She had lost the delights of her younger years *(Gen.20)*. Nevertheless, King Abimelech wanted her, he wanted her close by, and Sarah's husband dropped her into his hand.

What embarrasses one most for Abraham's sake is that he did not detect the deceit in his bosom, for he did not consider Sarah a holy temple, consecrated, set apart, being prepared by God, according to God's word *(Gen.18:14)*, for a miracle conception to take place within the next three months. It does appear not to have bothered him that insemination by Abimelech was not only an odious matter but a dangerous thwarting of God's intentions. In actual fact he, Abraham, was only but professing to be a man of faith!! He had publicly built altars and sacrificed to a Holy Sovereign God, but within the skins of his tent dwellings and behind his closed front door, his intentions and actions showed another colour. Abraham was willing to have the semen of another man, a heathen, enter and pollute Sarah's body within the particular period of three months. Again to save his many goats.

He brazenly insulted the Most High. Annihilation, instant death striking from the hand of God did not occur to him, as long as he was safe and sound and agreeably compatible with the peoples of Gerar. There was only one way of obtaining their favour. Sarah! If they perish by the hand of these 'foreigners' then it would include Ishmael, his heir. Disaster could be avoided and the beauty of Sarah was an asset, a trump in the palm of his hand. She was the shield to hold up against any potential threat *(Gen.12:11-13, 20:9-13)*. It had worked before, why not again?

Heathen King Abimelech proves himself way ahead of prophet Abraham—God speaks to him in a dream and he immediately responds to the urgent warning: hands off Sarah! He saw the terrible thing that almost took place. He saw right through the man Abraham, prophet of God. All of it was, to him and everyone reading Genesis, to say the least, despicable.

But God came to Abimelech in a dream by night, and said to him, Behold, thou art but a dead man, for the woman which thou hast taken; for she is a man/s wife

Then Abimelech called Abraham, and said unto him, What hast thou done unto us? and what have I offended thee, that thou hast brought on me and on my kingdom a great sin? Thou hast done deeds unto me that ought not to be done (Gen.20:3,9).

Evil Subterfuge

Abraham's excuses do not bear weight. He comes through in Scriptures as an exemplary man. This was for him a turbulent time; but in his predicament he does not exercise the faith we by traditional exegesis have accredited to him. Abraham does not display even a whisper of sturdy strength. He does not show by his actions he believes God would keep His word; that God could and would protect His covenants and promise of many nations through Sarah and himself.

He sought to bring about preservation of himself and his empire by hiding behind the skirts of his wife. Again Sarah's beauty had to do the job, at her cost and to his gain.

This is the danger of knowing the difference between good and evil: God had made His promises to Abraham, and he, seeing impending calamity, chooses not to rest in a faithful promise-keeping Father to work succour. He chooses rather to believe The Lie of circumstantial evidence and work out deliverance for himself.

And afterwards Abimelech wants to know: 'Goodness, man, whatever for?!'

Now why would Abraham disregard the power and the omniscience of God to extricate them from a displeasing physical and dangerous spiritual situation? (Don't we all look at things unpleasant and say we are 'under the circumstances?')

A stronghold *(11 Cor.10:3,4)* is a hornets' nest of reasoning and feelings, of fretting and broodings, all built on imagination and assumptions. We keep these thoughts going without investigation and pulling down, until eventually all becomes part of one's personality and life. Man would be shocked if he could gaze objectively on the private arena in his head.

Satan is, and always will be, a liar and he plan advances according to the fortresses man has permitted him to build in the mind. So? Why not use Abraham himself? Just make the man desperate; let him begin to wonder if he really heard from God. Begin to whisper into his ear: you're in foreign country, there are swarms of them about, and you'll lose everything you have, also Ishmael! Let him begin to fear. Disturb his so-called faith! Bring in a little bit of doubt. And then you have got him!

The devil knew should his strategy with Ishmael fail he would need a fresh one immediately shifting into first gear because he could never really know what God would be doing next ...

Satan had a plot enfolding, a ripe luscious apple dangling and ready for the picking. If a rank outsider, a total heathen, could impregnate Sarah within the crucial three-month period, the Seed to come would be supplanted by another impostor and the plan of God to save the human race once again be averted. What a cleverly detailed coup d'etat to rob humanity of Salvation!

Abraham blatantly ignored the protection God offers by faith—his Almighty God Who could save him, and Ishmael, his riches, his Sarah, Who could do so with one single word! Instead, he had swallowed The Lie, hook, line and sinker. He accepted the compensation Abimelech offered without blushing and without remonstrating against the deserved rebuke. Abraham wasn't in shallow waters, but in a muddy whirlpool of fear, of unbelief and disobedience.

In spite of the code of conduct in his day, his peers probably regarded Abraham as a man of God, and one would have thought maintaining this image alone would have kept him from falling into the Godless ways of those around him. A disappointing hero indeed—but for the grace of God—

Popular Conceptions Revised

Why do believers persist in thinking of Abraham and other highly esteemed Bible figures as different because God had dealt directly with them, and they should therefore be placed on a pedestal, deserving or not? Are we not inclined to attribute more to their characters than they inherently possessed?

The Bible throughout gives account of God dealing with ordinary human beings. Those who have by His grace accepted the undeserved gift of the Indwelling Christ, have also received a stand on the same Divine platform, but 'walking by revelation' makes the difference. Abraham was a man of the same substance as the next man, with the same human inclinations. I, for instance, can place personal honesty on a high premium and lose out on other spiritual matters requiring meticulous attention, yet Father God suffers all of us to be His children, albeit rebirthed and at times so recalcitrant.

Likely something of his lesson had rubbed off on Prophet Abraham for it struck him that intercessory prayer was called for. A high level historically and traditionally has always been associated with him and yet one cannot be sure of Abraham's motives or his level of understanding in these passages, because consistent and penetrating intercessory prayer rests on an intimate and unbroken walk with God.

On one hand does the prayer born of despair instantly connect with the Divine source of all assistance. The cataclysmic event of Sodom and Gomorrah and Abraham interceding is one amazing and encouraging instance *(Gen. 18)*. The Father responds even if the cry comes from the vilest for He is not a respecter of persons. His availability is as quick as a flash of lightning.

On the other hand, experience has repeatedly taught that repentance and restitution is the gateway to answered prayer. What went on in Abraham's mind when he prayed for the restoration of Abimilech's house? This prayer is not recorded, but he had started praying for the King of Gerar's wife and his female slaves for the Lord had on account of Sarah, closed fast the wombs of all in the king's household and they were healed.

Now unto him that is able to do exceeding abundantly above all that we ask or think, according to the power that worketh in us (Eph.3:20).

With God, there is no such thing as coincidence. Had the penny at last dropped? With Abraham praying for other barren women, his own wife is touched and his relationship with Abimelech deepened, for subsequently they agreeably made contract. But Abraham was cornered. He could not but recognize the fact—sin against God lay in his bosom, and it befouled many. He had been the cause of the blight.

Our walk with God and our measure of faith does not depend on what others do or don't do, but entirely upon what we do with what our Father wants us to do. Abraham had made so many mistakes, yet all was not over for him. He had believed in God and it was counted to him as righteousness *(Gen. 15:6)*. For God, His child had learned the lesson and the score was settled, for Abraham his 'forty-year trek' was almost over—and Sarah conceived, miraculously.

8

THE MOVE OF GOD UPON MAN

Who's Spiritual Influence?

Satan knows the spiritual influence of woman upon man is a threat to him. He merely has to bend the quality of the influence, slightly. Tip it a bit; keep it as close as possible to the truth, well camouflaged. He had a very good start in the Garden of Eden for he could use Eve. And Sarah. And he has done so with millions of other women ever since.

Woman—is she not wondrously equipped for this essential, this fundamental move of God upon Man? What is she doing with it?

God deemed it fit to raise Himself a new Sarah who would stand fast and hold to her new found convictions, for Satan never ceases his attempts to demolish any structure resisting and holding ground against him. Sarah was adamant that Abraham's tents not be divided by the presence of Ishmael and his mother from Egypt.

Every kingdom divided against itself is brought to desolation, and a house divided against a house falleth (Luk.11:17,18).

Abram who, birthed by the Spirit, became Abraham, represents the male sex. He stands for truth and testimony and justification by faith. **Faith is the objective.**

The female sex is represented by Sarai, who became 'beautiful princess, one who reigns (queen). She is Sarah and stands for experience, life and obedience. **Obedience is subjective.**

Clearly then, **Sarah** (Single-Couple-Church-Bride) **represents the subjective work of the Lord upon mankind.**

It is important to understand this, for it clarifies the fundamental and proven principle of submission and obedience as based on a spiritual foundation established in Jesus Christ. Error is clear in the unregenerate concept of 'wifely sub-mission'—and most unfortunate.

The Mystery Of Marriage

This is a great mystery, but I speak concerning Christ and the Church (Eph.5:32)

But I would have you know, that the head of every man is Christ; and the head of the woman is the man; and the head of Christ is God. (Col.3:23,24).

Wives, submit yourselves unto your own husbands, as unto the Lord (Eph.5:22).

But he that is joined unto the Lord is one spirit (l Cor.6:17),

And whatever ye do, do it heartily, as to the Lord, and not unto men; Knowing that of the Lord ye shall receive the reward of the inheritance; for ye serve the Lord Christ Col.3:23,24).

What is read into these verses makes the meaningful changes in a personal approach to, and appreciation of marriage, and an entirely different light falls on marriage when the **subjective work of God on man, as channelled through a godly woman, becomes clear.**

The influence of Sarai on Abram, and then Sarah on Isaac, differed in essence and in fruit. Hardly anywhere else in Scriptures do we receive more lucid information on submission and obedience than contained in the chronicles of Abraham and Sarah.

No Place For Hesitation

At the appointed time and according to the word of God, Sarah gave birth to Isaac, considered the fruit of a spiritual marriage.

Inner quality is revealed by the quality of laughter—with the realization of God's promise to her, Sarah's laughter has another ring to it *(Gen.21:6)*. One translation, though, gives the impression that ninety-year-old Sarah felt ridiculous. Fear of 'what other people are saying' keeps one fettered. Lingering in, and permitting smirches to stick to the mind, (as if such misery will bring one into the holiness and purity required for any task ahead), is not of the Holy Spirit.

Sarah now has reason to lay aside the shame of barrenness, of the dry unproductive periods in her life, of discouraging inter-personal relationships, of past sins, and last but not least, of disobedience.

It may seem callous that the bondwoman and her son was no longer acceptable and had to be cast out, but no teaching could be as serious, or more important, than committed single-minded purpose in practicing this principle.

Tell me, ye that desire to be under the law, do ye not fear the law?

For it is written, that Abraham had two sons, the one by a bondmaid, the other by a freewoman.

But he who was of the bondwoman was born after the flesh; but he of the freewoman was by promise.

Which things are an allegory: for these are the two covenants; the one from the mount Sinaii, which gendereth to bondage, which is Agar.

For this Agar is mount Sinai, in Arabia, and answereth to Jerusalem which now is, and is in bondage with her children.

But Jerusalem which is above is free, which is the mother of us all.

For it is written, Rejoice, thou barren that bearest not; break forth and cry, thou that travailest not; for the desolate hath many more children than she which hath an husband.

Now we, brethren, as Isaac was, are the children of promise

But when he that was born after the flesh persecuted him that was born after the Spirit, even so it is now

Nevertheless what saith the scripture? Cast out the bondwoman and her son: for the son of the bondwoman shall not be heir with the son of the freewoman

So then brethren, we are not children of the bondswoman, but of the free (Gal.4:21-31).

Thus natural for Ishmael to feel the loss of prominence and shine. This is typical of human nature: take your frustrations out on punch-bag number one. Fourteen years of position and favour and then having to see the promising future that was so effortlessly going to fall into your lap being phased out like early mist before the sun and all because of one small infant!

How many would have reacted differently; inflicting emotional abuse on the defenceless, a gleeful if vicious nip on the backside, a heckling jab between the blades (when you think no one sees you), all instigated by disappointment and envy. Badgering young Isaac was so gratifying that Ishmael could not constrain himself and to refuse the temptation to mock and taunt was just too much to ask. Sarah had had enough. She had developed the courage of her newfound convictions and was drawing her boundaries. She was not going to take the bullying any longer.

Would that all Sarah's come to this point! There is no reason for Spirit-born, Blood-washed saints to put up with demonic harassment. This is a limitless subject for searching discussion but suffice it to say, unless we come into first-hand knowledge of the modus operandi of the enemy, our ignorance and lack of vigilance all too often finds one at the receiving end. There is no place in spiritual warfare for hesitation, passivity, or compromise.

And Sarah saw the son of Hagar the Egyptian which she had born unto Abraham, mocking

Wherefore she said unto Abraham, Cast out this bondwoman and her son; for the son of this bondwoman shall not be heir with my son, even with Isaac. And the thing was very grievous in Abrahams's sight because of his son.

And God said unto Abraham, Let it not be grievous in thy sight because of the lad, and because of the bondwoman: in all that Sarah hath said unto thee, hearken unto her voice; for in Isaac shall thy seed be called (Gen.219-12).

Here we have it. Not by implication, not by speculation, but by the Holy Spirit. One plain statement, in fact, a command. **In all that Sarah has said to you, do what she asks, for in Isaac shall your posterity be called.** *(Rom.9:7).* So let us sit up and really hear what the Spirit of God is saying, because from this moment on, Sarah comes into her rightful heritage, completely into the will of God Who has decreed that she shall be a mother of nations, with kings coming form her.

Egypt, Hagar, and Ishmael represent a world of evil, sin and the flesh. They represent a decomposed outer shell of dead works and corrupt selfishness I-Me-Mine (old man of the flesh) does not lightly discard. It takes a wilderness, cutting truth, and searing Light for us to see ourselves. Hagar and Sarah each had this experience—a supernatural visitation, each in her own personal desolation.

When the Angel of the Lord gently bid pregnant Hagar return to a destructive situation in the tents of Abraham, her submssion included another 16 years odd of misery and emotional suffering—for both women. In the wilderness Hagar had been permitted to **see** *(Gen.16:13)* **but chose to keep her face turned toward Egypt.** She took her son into what she herself was at core, and eventually took him back with her whence she had come.

This is where, when and how we play god in our lives and in those of our children. Sarah, when cutting comprehension fell on her own particular wilderness, chose the Light and, together with her son, walked straight into it. The Ashes of the red heifer *(Num.19)* was assured, guaranteed, and certain—the only hope for a dying world.

Magnificently, she steps into place, and into the purpose of God's move on mankind. *Gen.24:67* clinches the spiritual culmination and from this last verse of Chapter 24, Sarah is not mentioned again—she dies to our reading of Genesis until such time as her physical death when Abraham, at great cost and effort, obtains a suitable place of burial. He would have his bones lay with hers. They had indeed become one.

Stepping Perfectly Into

Sarah's life and laughter lay in the Spirit of the true Israel. *Gen.21:12* reveals an astounding development, the crux of everything God expects of husband and wife: **unity.**

How amazing for God to instruct Abraham *to submit* to Sarah in all pertaining the child Isaac. Of his many riches, his most treasured gem was to be returned to the spiritual womb of the woman whom he held in such low esteem he could sell her out to appease the lusts of other men as a means of saving himself.

The tables had indeed turned. For a Hebrew of Abraham's stature and standing, this is exceptional, most extraordinary. What is behind this move of God? The severity with which males held women subordinate in those times, one can say, the obsessive preoccupation with submission and submissiveness, has in one verse simply been brushed aside. It would seem God could not trust Abraham with this charge—something of such extreme importance is contained in these verses that no seriously committed believer dare disregard it. On closer examination we come to the gist of what God had said to Adam, and is now saying through Abraham and Sarah.

Abraham was to listen to Sarah in all concerning her son Isaac: her influence was brought to bear on a small boy—who was born remarkably, according to the promise *(Gal.4:29),* who would grow in grace beyond his years, and later be led by the faith of his father to an altar as a living sacrifice to God Almighty.

Abraham would still go through a fire of torment and vehemently oppose everything Sarah would employ to rid their lives of what was a stench to the nostrils of God. And Sarah is not mentioned by historians as partaker of suffering! Often His voice was not heard, but this time Sarah did. Every Spirit-filled saint has at some time or another experienced God not making a move without first speaking to His child. Oh yes, she heard Him ... she stood firm and resolute. She was the mother of the real heir, and **all that is not part of Father God's original intentions for Man must be removed.** Spiritual preparation of Isaac was to take place and she was the only appointed and filled vessel to accomplish the task. For this reason her husband was to send his private idol packing to the wilderness, and assist his wife in the responsibility of raising a Spirit-child. Profound.

If inclined to ignore Adam's mission, then be reminded of the similarity with Abraham's mission—they were to walk and live habitually before Almighty God, and be without blame. Perfect, whole-hearted, complete. Furthermore, God had made pledge with Abraham and physical circumcision sealed the pledge, marking his descendants as being distinct from other races.

Of cardinal importance was Sarah's supportive contribution to the quality of Abraham's walk. This would closely affect Isaac with whom this covenant, promise and pledge would later be established *(Gen. 17:21)*. However, the blessing promised would forthwith come upon the Gentiles *so that we through faith might (all) receive the (realisation of) the promise of the (Holy) Spirit* and **circumcision of the heart now marks the spiritual descendants of Abraham as being distinct from the peoples of the world** *(Rom.2:28,29, Col.2:9-11)*.

Sarah's obedience to the spiritual head of her family is to yield to the Voice of God speaking through him.

And this is Sarah in submission: her persuasive influence exerted on the spiritual head, tactfully, lovingly, without duplicity, effectively engineering and, delivering the goods.

How?

She does it in the power of the Holy Spirit, letting go of hidden lusts and secret sins, ridding their marriage of pollution, resolutely throwing out of her husband's tents all that stains and stinks. The junk in thinking processes, (so easily transmitted to small children who have not yet reached the age of discernment and decision-making); superfluous glitter and clutter in her environment, everything redundant and all spelling spiritual death, she deals with mercilessly.

When the welfare of Isaac as heir of the Kingdom is in jeopardy she takes a firm stand, and Abraham is to submit. Sarah walks in close communion with the Lord, and instantly detects a false note creeping into the word her husband brings. This is a major instance where her persuasive influence is the protective element. When the husband does hear God speaking to him, Sarah can confidently rest in his measure of faith and so they both enter the Sabbath rest of God. Abraham will be with her wholeheartedly where she instructs, teaches and leads her brood by her example, in the divine ways of God.

Contamination! Continuous scrubbing has to be done. Touch dirt, just but flirt with sin, and the smell of it clings to your person. The stench of filth harboured in your tents is pervasive and should you inhale it, the foulness becomes an anaesthetic—be rid of compromising complacency or it will have you fast asleep. Sarah had no need to be told this because everything Ishmael represented, spelled danger.

Do not tread on the toes of an unsaved without wearing full armour!

Sarah knew Egypt within her home would seize every opportunity to get at the heir should she drop her vigilance. The unsaved cannot inherit together with a true child of the Father; he cannot savour the things of the Kingdom and the Spirit; he wears soiled linen; he smells of death and carries it with him; Egypt subversively and continuously attempts to usurp the place of Jesus.

Causing To Let Fall

Abraham did not find it easy to let go of the foreign idol in his heart.

There is compassion for him as he pleads for the son of his disobedience, but here was no way out for him but relinquish Ishmael and expel him and his mother to the wilderness *(Gen.21)*.

This outstanding woman was no longer a carnal, jealous and vengeful Sarai attempting cruel riddance of a human threat to her peace and position *(Gen.16:1-16,)* but a prophetic Sarah who would not permit demonic activity in the vicinity of the heir entrusted to her care. Sarah tightened her tent pegs *(Is.54:1-5)*.

This testing of Abraham, and his subsequent victory over personal sentiments, was a further setback to the strategy of the Serpent.

When Abraham submitted to, and obeyed the voice of God, Sarah could come into full Godly submission to her husband. His faith and testimony formed a protective shield of support, thus safely releasing his wife into the ministry for which God had equipped and separated her.

Interaction on this level works on a triangular basis between the Lord and each of the spouses; a very high standard of mutual submission and obedience, and not comprehended by the carnal thinking in terms of the physical. Unity of this calibre produces 'many nations and kings'—revival as understood by those who have actually seen and experienced the Holy Spirit sweeping over individuals, whole congregations and countries, bringing hundreds and thousands of souls to salvation.

That they all may be one; as thou, Father, art in me, and I in thee, that they also may be one in us: that the world may believe that thou hast sent me.

And the glory which thou gavest me I have given them; that they may be one, even as we are one,

I in them, and thou in me, that they may be made perfect in one; and that the world may know that thou hast sent me, and hast loved them, as thou hast loved me (Joh.17:21-23).

But Abraham was still wrestling before God, holding on to Ishmael—his own interests and idols. To have God rebuke the Enemy for us, we first have to relinquish our Ishmaels and sentence them to the desert, where a merciful Father, being the One to judge, will deal effectively with all that intrudes. We can only sacrifice a trueborn on the altar of faith for God to produce many nations and kings unto Himself.

The principle of multiplicity on a spiritual level is clear

9

GOD'S PURPOSE

A Man And His Son

The ring of Abraham's laughter had cause for change: the inexorable Voice of testing sent him into the mountains *(Gen.22)*.

The time for sowing his seed of faith had come. Would his faith be true and pure enough? Only our Father in heaven can gauge the measure of faith of the individual. For Abraham there was no escape. Impossible for us to attempt any description of what went on in this father's mind and perhaps we should leave it to the imagination of other fathers? When reading secular trash, we either gratify a submerged hunger for cruelty and obscenity, or we only skim the surface of unpleasant events, or choose to skip it entirely as if non-existent. But when we read the Bible, we have to take note of every sentence even if it appears strange and totally out of order.

In *Gen.13:16* the promise to Abraham with regard to his seed was earthy, 'dust to dust'. But in *Gen.15:4-6* some years later, the promise refers to the spiritual Seed through Abraham's loins: *Look now toward heaven, and tell the stars, if thou be able to number them.* And then consider this: not until I myself have to make a crucial and agonizing choice between God and my son, can I know anything about putting myself in Abraham's shoes, identify with his doubts and questioning, feel the fear and the pain, have some idea of the remarkable degree of faith he at last had come to exercise. He had to sacrifice his precious son on an altar to ensure the birth of countless souls into Christ.

In *Hebrews 11:17-19* we get some idea of what is at the core of *Gen.21:12, and Gen.22:1-10*. By faith Abraham was put to the test. He had accepted God's promises and was not only willing, but ready to sacrifice Isaac, his only son, through whom his descendants would be reckoned. Now he had already brought Isaac for an offering. Abraham reasoned, and firmly believed, that God was able to raise him up from among the dead. Abraham's test lay in taking young Isaac up that mountain, and going through the whole ritual of preparing an altar, getting his son down on it, and raising his knife. In this sense, Isaac was figuratively dead, so he actually did receive him back from the dead.

Indeed, in my unregenerate state I would have refused to even try and understand the whole business—I would say that I was being expected to perform spiritual acrobatics—. yet, the absence of the obvious makes one keen to examine every unfolding detail.

We come as far as *Ch.23* and have many questions to raise about Sarah and Isaac for not a single word depicts their faith and their fellowshipping with God, which make their contribution to history all the more conspicuous. God also is silent … or the chronicler finds the subject far too profound for commonplace words.

Surely, with the Lord in control, mother and son would both have extraordinary vision and courage, but being simple people, they would also have their human trepidations and emotions. Different sources speculate on the age of young Isaac, and it can safely be assumed he was no toddler for he was loaded with the necessary kindle. Neither could Abraham at his ripe old age, physically have lifted a full-grown youth onto the altar. ***He had to get onto it by himself.***

The role Isaac plays warrants time spent on his development. Anything still hidden in the inner man, perhaps secret pride on being selected and becoming 'the high father' of many nations all had to be scorched off. What was displeasing to God had to be consumed by flames and for this sole purpose, Abraham's 'Laughter' (meaning of the name Isaac) was to go up in smoke. Isaac carried the wood for the sacrifice on his back up the mountain; Calvary may not be as high, but the Cross was much, much heavier … If there was any dross left in this father's heart, then God certainly dealt with it when the last seconds came and he had his final moment of decision. Abraham chose God, and lifted his hand to slit the throat of his son. Blood was called for, and blood had to flow, freely.

Isaac! How old was he when this drama unfolded? What was the calibre of his steel? Who of us will meekly place himself on an altar for slaughter? Who will extend both wrists and be bound and trussed willingly for such extreme sacrifice? Can I climb onto that altar in my own strength and with my personal convictions, lay myself down by free choice, without fear or objection against my father's will for me? What did I read in my mother's eyes as we said farewell before undertaking this journey? How strong must my faith be in a God who makes promises, far beyond human comprehension, for me to arduously carry sufficient wood for a pyre up a bleak desert mountain on the word of my dad? And that God will provide the sacrifice? And when I understand that my own person is the offering, not rebel in shocked disillusionment and make a desperate bid for freedom? How sure can I be my father really did hear a God commanding him to sacrifice me? ME?!!

What manner of man was Isaac? He could not meekly and voluntarily have permitted his father to bind him to the altar. Who can accurately describe the emotional condition of this father and his young son? There was an influence, either a Satanic soporific or a direct supernatural working of God on these two men. Could it have been a strong interplay of soul force? To my own spirit, the Holy Spirit declares emphatically 'NO!' This was of God!

No human planning could have produced the exact climate. Human resources were not permitted to jell into anxious impulsiveness: 'Let me get on with the job and be done!' No devilish interference could have precipitated the final and fatal slash on that exposed throat, only Divine power could have stayed the hand of Abraham in the crucial moment. Flippancy is uncalled for here, but I do know, if I were Isaac, I would have resisted those binding thongs with teeth, nails, fists and feet, and probably have socked my father one in the gut as well. I would have sped down the mountain like a hare, screaming inanely for something abnormal have me vanish, removed instantly to the uttermost corner of earth!

A Mother And Her Son

The only logical conclusion is that Isaac was of spiritual substance, a man seeing in the far future another Man strung up on a Cross. Isaac's submission was God-inspired, nothing there of mere bravado or admirable human courage.

Spiritual preparation, a profound inner conviction, and a transforming intellectual understanding of the Divine requisite for sacrificial blood, could only have been instilled with mother's milk and fed over the years of infancy and early childhood. Isaac, born of the Spirit, knew supernaturally what it would cost The Father to sacrifice His only Son Who loved the lost so much He would give Himself for us. Isaac was prepared and free to give himself and in one singular, tremendous flash when the will of father and son converged in perfect submission, the demands of God was met and He by His power instantly provided a substitute sacrifice. A ram caught in a bush. The faith of Abraham was justified, the obedience and submission of Abraham and Sarah united in spirit, was justified. Jesus Christ could continue His way down the ages right up to the perfect timing of the crucifixion, and enter our sick and bleeding hearts at Calvary, His righteousness henceforth counted as ours.

When will we ever *really* learn about submission?

Beautiful mother Sarah's knees, at which Isaac sat, is the Gamaliel *(Acts 22:31)* of all sincere believers. From the loins of Isaac would come Jacob the Pretender, who some years later wrestled before God and also birthed into new life. He became Pure-of-Heart and he is called Israel, the New Testament designation for all Christians who have had a vital overcoming experience.

Sarah is the prototype of every mother who would give her submission to God's order absolute priority and quality consideration. Who would raise children of single-minded purpose, believers who have come to recognise the disabling corruption of the evil tree as self-centred independence and who will not lift a hand to partake of it. They know to discipline themselves and work out their own salvation.

Only to the extent that we are taught from early infancy about the Self as an idol in the middle of the garden of which the fruit are not to be eaten, can we become the garden of the Lord Jesus Christ. He alone should have full and free access *(Songs 4:16)*.

Much emphasis is placed on building a healthy self-image and mothers are treading dangerous ground in this respect if they have no sound knowledge of *Rom.Chs.5-8*. Most lack the required diligence, or dedication, for a spiritual journey of excellence with their children. The more we learn of the Indwelling Christ, the more acute the desire is to become less in own estimation. Indeed a narrow gate, but the power released by denial of I-Me-Mine is a serious consideration, and then we are not talking about self-effacement, however heroic towards the cause of the Kingdom, if it is an effort of the flesh. Distinction between the two is there, and one knows it in the heart.

A 40-year detour through the desert, as did the Israelites, can be avoided if the things of God and His Son are received in mother's milk. Isaac was ready for weaning at the approximate age of three; could be this was physical only, but not entirely, considering he was born remarkably and according to the working of the Holy Spirit. John, the Baptist, also an ordinary person, was filled and moved by the Holy Spirit even before he was born.

The preparation of Isaac enabled him to lay himself down as sacrifice without demurring—and God could intervene miraculously and virtually raise him from the dead to keep the line of the Saviour intact, on our behalf.

Why do we hesitate? Why not positively and firmly take hold of God's promises? By grace alone are we granted access to a Spirit-filled life; let us avail ourselves of it and by example teach our children the Truth—and they will lay their lives down at His feet and walk His Way, supernaturally, joyously and victoriously.

10

THE UNPURGED HEART

Ezekiel

We think of our indiscretions as something that just happened—so sorry about it—but Ezekiel sees much further. He prophesied from captivity in Babylon.

Babylon—being in bondage. We can be committed to Jesus and still be continuously harassed and assailed. The prophet addresses not only those with a seared conscience, but warns the saints—we think we stand when in fact we are beginning to topple, and may be horrified to wake up and find ourselves back in captivity.

He describes God's dealings with him as severe and without consideration for his person. Ezekiel, always concerned for the honour of God, deserves to be placed in a class distinctly his own and what he has to say earns respect.

And he put forth the form of an hand, and took me by a lock of mine head; and the spirit lifted me up between the earth and the heaven, and brought me in the visions of God to Jerusalem, to the door of the inner gate that looketh toward the north; where was the seat of the image of jealousy, which provoketh to jealousy.

And, behold, the glory of the God if Israel was there, according to the vision that I saw in the plain.

Then he said unto me, Son of man, lift up thine eyes now the way toward the north. So I lifted up mine eyes the way toward the north, and behold northward at the gate of the altar this image of jealousy in the entry.

He said furthermore unto me, Son of man, seest thou what they do? Even the great abominations that the house of Israel committeth here, that I should go far off from my sanctuary? But turn thee yet again, and thou shalt see greater abominations. And he brought me to the door of the court; and when I looked, behold a hole in the wall.

Then he said unto me, Son of man, dig now in the wall: and when I had digged in the wall, behold a door.

And he said unto me, Go in, and behold the wicked abominations that they do here.

So I went in and saw; and behold every form of creeping things, and abominable beasts, and all the idols of the house of (Israel, pourtrayed upon the wall round about.

And there stood before them seventy men of the ancients of the house of Israel, and in the midst of them stood Jaazamiah the son of Shaplan, with every man his censer in his hand; and a thick cloud of incense went up.

Then said he unto me, Son of man, hast thou seen what the ancients of the house of Israel do in the dark, every man in the chambers of his imagery? for they say The Lord seeth us not; the Lord hath forsaken the earth. (Ezek.8:3-12).

Seeing things from man's perspective brings about mistakes in judgment, but here Ezekiel is giving God's perspective (:3). The divided heart, unpurged, is shown—demons and the presence of God together in the same temple.

Good and evil in the same tent! When the prophet knocked a hole through the wall, a shut door behind it was revealed—abominable, hidden things of evil being committed by those who are thought to be blameless in their Christian walk, are taking on unprecedented proportions. God, Who sees me in the secret place, will also judge me in the secret place, and the people around me won't even know—

Then said he unto me, Son of man, hast thou seen what the ancients of the house of Israel do in the dark, every man in the chambers of his imagery? For they say the Lord seeth us not; the Lord hath forsaken the earth.

He said also unto me, Turn thee yet again, and thou shalt see greater abominations that they do. Then he brought me to the door of the gate of the Lord's house which was toward the north, and behold, there sat women weeping for Tammuz (Ezek.8:13,14).

Semiramus and her son Nimrod were worshipped as sacred gods in ancient Babylonia. Tammuz is the child born of their incestuous relationship, yet Semiramus claimed that she had conceived supernaturally. The mother-son cult is a pagan stronghold and can best be described as broad and catholic (the word catholic meaning all-embracing, *'brëë algemene'*) A Spirit of Religion was carried to the people on the back of the golden calf *(Ex.32)*. Tammuz their child is the hidden evil directly connected with masked whoredom. In *Ez.32:6* the people offered sacrifices to the golden calf, as if unto God, on the word of Aaron (:5). Then they ate, drank, and 'got up to play.' Tammuz was known as the god of sex orgies. A gold ring with a small cross is the emblem of Tammuz and worn mostly as earrings; and popular with some today

In *Ex.3:21,22* God instructed the Israelite women to spoil the Egyptians and place all on their sons and daughters before leaving Egypt. In *Ex.32*, however, the gold earrings were taken from the ears of all the people and from it came forth the golden calf—and we wonder at the prevailing decadence, whoredom, gross incest, rape, pornography, lechery, and the increase of gold earrings with the emblem of Tammuz worn in these days by both sexes, whether sound, lesbian, or homosexual.

Whoredom! It is what the Israelites wanted. It is what most people want today. And it is what many mothers, perhaps unwittingly, condone and put on their children—they weep for Tammuz at the doors of the temples.

Alarmingly, a large percentage of women know full well what they are doing. God is, through the writings of Ezekiel, describing evil activities manifesting through females.

These cannot be described as merely silly women, simple and gullible, as Paul wrote in his second letter and third chapter to Timothy, who is to understand that in the last days there will set in perilous times of great stress and trouble. It will be hard to deal with, and hard to bear, for people will have become utterly self-centred. They will be lovers of money and have an inordinate greed for wealth; they will be proud, arrogant and insolent.

Paul says that they will have an abusive set of mind, disobedient to parents and authority; ungrateful, unholy and profane. They will be without normal affection, but callous, inhuman, relentless, and refuse to live in peace. They will be slanderers, accusing falsely and making trouble; intemperate and loose in morals and conduct, uncontrolled and fierce, and haters of good.

People will be treacherous, rash and inflated with self-conceit. They will be lovers of sensual pleasures and vain amusements more than loving God.

Furthermore, in the last days, people will show themselves as being religious, but at the same time they deny and reject the power of true Godliness. They do not know the power of God. Their conduct belies the genuineness of what they profess. Timothy is instructed to avoid all such, and simply turn away from them.

Paul states furthermore that some of these worm their way into homes and charm silly, weak-natured, gullible women who are burdened with sin, and are easily seduced and led into evil doings.

These silly women are *ever learning, and never able to come to the knowledge of the truth (2 Tim.3:7).*

Nothing is covered that shall not be revealed. A final heart-searching will take place before the last judgment. Overcomers will be further purified; consuming coals of fire and the cleansing of lips will take place. Every Christian will experience the probing, and the conviction of all (the slightest detail included) the rubbish accumulated over years; words indiscriminately uttered will be held as indisputable evidence.

Do We Begin Again?

Yes. Let us return to our first love. And where do we begin?

Consider Sarah's purposeful decisions. She no longer nursed any doubts about her worth—she had an heir to nurture. She would protect him to the uttermost from anything illegitimate. She had set herself to completing her task. This is not sermonizing, nor is it a self-betterment plan of action, but if we are going to enter Sarah's tent then we, having been birthed into Jesus should repeatedly take stock.

Begin by asking the Holy Spirit to point out things normally considered as small and apparently unimportant, those innocuous little things appealing to a sense of our own importance.

Then on to analysing one's *motives* and courageously deal with the relating issue if a sense of embarrassment makes one squirm, (ignore it and the lesson will be repeated with severity.)

In a sense, I am a slave of that to which I yield. If I am a slave of I-Me-Mine then I must know the Lord does not mix His Self with my self and it grieves Him to anger when I take it for granted that He acquiescently shares my temple with demons. **For by whatever any one is made inferior or overcome or worsted, to that person or thing he is enslaved** *(2 Pet.2:19b)*.

A true Sarah knows that in the street where she lives and walks and raises her children there is a Way of walking before the Father.

Take note of your casual words—what do you chatter about? There are four points to cultivate—stop talking for the sake of saying something; keeping quiet; listening and *really hearing;* and, saying only what should be said.

If we desire to be one of Sarah's company we will also commit ourselves to the principle of submission to authority appointed by God. Obedience to the Lord *only* should be the springboard of our motives and subsequent conduct, and we shall experience in a hundred practical ways how the Lord is our covering, our backing, and our strength in overcoming.

Whatever the task is that I have been set I must work at it with my whole being as if I am doing it for the Lord and not for men.

I know I will receive my reward from the Lord and not from men for it is the Lord Jesus Christ that I am actually serving

He who deals wrongfully will reap the fruit of his folly and receive punishment because no matter what a person's position may be, slave or master, there is no favouritism with God *(Col.3:23-25)*.

Not with eyeservice as menpleasers, but as the servants of Christ, doing the will of God from the heart;

With good will doing service as to the Lord and not to men;
Knowing that whatsoever good thing any man doeth, the same shall he receive from the Lord, whether he be bond or free (Eph.6:6-8)
For whether we live, we live unto the Lord; and whether we die, we die unto the Lord: whether we live therefore, or die, we are the Lord's (Rom..14:8).

Therefore, if we know in our spirit that the authority is self-appointed and off-track, then our commitment to submission does not apply in that case to the authority. Then we '**put on' our service as unto the Lord** the same as we do with our armour *(Eph.6:10-20).* Unfair? Yes. Someone usually pays the price for another's authoritarian presumptuousness! This is a tall order and it takes faith to submit, but the Lord can then start driving in the nails where the devil does not want it driven. What we did to Jesus was unspeakably unfair but He had a vision; He knew what His mission was, and the ultimate goal. Submission is a service unto the Lord, a sacrifice of yourself, and a call to partake of the impossible. *For with God nothing is ever impossible, and no word from God shall be without power or impossible of fulfilment*

Then Mary said, Behold, I am the handmaiden of the Lord; let it be done to me according to what you have said (Luk.1:37,38)

Just How Serious?

Subjecting yourself to any form and degree of unfairness is debatable. The rebellious can stop fighting with the unfairness spouted by a 'prejudiced' Paul for we have been set free from the bondage into which Adam and Eve had fallen. The Lord is leading every Godly couple into a fresh measure of understanding—He is beckoning them to partake of closer intimacy with Him.

Sarah represents the influence of the Lord upon man. She also represents reborn couples walking in such righteousness and agreement of spirit that they can mother new believers into birthing. And for the reborn married woman who is not equally yoked, the issue at stake here is whether she is on a level of spiritual development where she knows her suffering is toward a work of God and not just pernicious demonic pestering to keep her from an unbroken walk with Jesus.

Obedience means a crucified life and this means nothing less than crucified appetites, whether it is desires of the soul hampering the ascendancy of the spirit, or merely avid flesh in its many guises. A parting shot in this respect would be to recognise the lusts and improper habits not yet disciplined—the range has no limit—call them blind spots, anything from bickering bouts in which I must have the last and final say, to the third and fourth compulsive mouthful of goodies just because it looks so good and tastes so good.

If you want to know more about yourself, then proven information is presented in *Is.58:3 through Is.59:14*. These passages throw light on fasting in the real sense of the word. Read it as if abstract and not presented as a guide for practical and physical application only, and you will be horrified at your previous responses to fasting.

Try yourself out on this one: see how long you can abstain from referring to yourself, thinking or talking about yourself, or promoting your own interests, however slight. An hour? Ten minutes, three?

Well now, am I in the habit of giving uncalled for advice, giving instructions on how the obvious should be done?

Am I a pot, and calling the kettle black? Do I dump my self-opinionated wisdom on others?

Do I embrace deceit by a mere nod of assent? Because this is participation in the deceitfulness of other hearts and makes mine as guilty.

Do I clothe or undress people by what I say or do not say?

Do I judge others and flatter myself by calling it the 'gift of discernment'?

The culmination of exhortative fasting is *Is.59:12,13*. To fast from what we normally take into our minds is on another level, if not higher, than a fast from food (what we normally take into our mouths so as to stuff our bellies) in order to draw nigh to God.

Have your family and friends jot down whatever they notice about **you,** when and where necessary and ask them to be sincere and frank. There is nothing complicated or shaming about accepting honest correction, and moving on to straightforward confession and genuine repentance. (Oh, would that I practice what I preach!!) *(1 Cor.9:27)*.

But do not be deceived if the flesh objects, for the Word always whips up the mind of the flesh into awareness of its rebellion and the flesh sure isn't going to like this treatment. Crossing the borderline into obedience is a Rubicon spelling misery and death, slow death. The reward? No one can tell, God alone knows.

Severe stringency is of the flesh, dead works. It robs the personality of spontaneous joy and vibrancy, whereas a crucified life and crucified appetites never quench the spirit but releases another expression of self. The call is to a supernatural walk with Him, not subservience to any man, and our major concern and an equally difficult discipline, should be in getting our Self out of His way.

There is to be no interference with God's order, from Governments down, to little me—the slightest twinge of rebellion spiritually concerning our spouse, or anyone else for that matter, will set progress into reverse. The serpent's venom will permeate your family and also resound within the radius of your fellowship and associates and set your world aflame. Knowledge of good and evil has us concentrating on our selves and not on the Father.

If wives and mothers do not really understand what Paul is getting at when he instructs women to be submissive to their husbands, they will be driven by the devourer to self-righteousness in a false expression of submission.

If you find your spiritual authority to be out of touch with what God is saying *to you*, what are you to do? A number of severe passages deal with this question. *1 Cor.5:6-13* is a shocking injunction: you *don't even eat with him!* What kind of food is meant here? Who and what kind of person is the Holy Spirit talking about?

If you do not 'submissively as you ought' appease a self-appointed religious spirit, you'll soon be accused you are in rebellion. Women have spiritual abilities not only equal, but often excelling those of men. This is why, and how *a woman shall compass a man (Jer.31:22)*.She is to take firm stand and exert influence when she knows God has spoken and confirmed His Word to her—she has then become the protector.

The one question of importance to settle with finality is, **just how serious am I with God?**

Decide what your intentions and expectations are concerning your children and eternity. Submission and obedience to God in what He alone expects of you, has Him taking care of your rebellion and subsequently of all governments and authorities you do not deem fit to exercise rule over you, inclusive of husbands spiritually out of focus. It does not mean difficult situations will conveniently evaporate, but rather, your own attitude will change and another frame of mind will handle anything unpalatable. Consider carefully when something appears to be 'another confirmation' that you are not being deceived, but at peaceful decision-making when seeking to do the will of God.

11

SARAH'S CHILDREN

Saying What Should Be Said

In *Ezek.8* the prophet is led by the Spirit to show the real heart-throb of Satan—a contaminated human bloodline on which evil thrives, born of, and raised by adulterous self-indulgent Woman, a lost posterity steeped in whoredom and passing their spiritual and physical diseases on to the next generation of susceptible weaklings.

Obviously, one cannot cover in a few pages the whole spectrum of the prevailing decadence. So unobtrusively are evil intentions woven into everyday life that we miss the power, the pace, the purposeful advance, and the practical, methodical way in which the devourer applies his scheming.

Young mothers are helplessly enmeshed in modern lifestyle because within themselves they have no other frame of reference. The mentality of our day has changed to the extent where we cannot clearly see the difference between Light and dark. Also, Satan knows we are in the end times; he doubles his fury daily, his time is short.

And so is ours.

God reveals through Ezekiel the appalling spirit-poverty and idolatry of man, hidden things in the closets of believers and non-believers. Decadent? The word stands for everything debased, degenerate, immoral, debauched, dissipated, obscene, smutty and vulgar.

Listen, and HEAR what the Spirit is saying, and exercise the common sense with which God has endued all His children. IF you have chosen the Way and will walk down Sarah's street, then it is imperative you read *Ezekiel 13* in as many translations as possible.

Ezekiel brings a harsh word.

It calls for loving, yet relentless courage to rebuke mothers who profess a birthing by the Spirit yet wilfully crosses the border into Egypt.

Again Jeremiah is saying it just as it is:

Righteous art thou O lord, when I plead with thee; yet let me talk with thee of thy judgments: Wherefore doth the way of the wicked prosper? Wherefore are all they happy that deal very treacherously!

Thou hast planted them, yea, they have taken root: they grow, yea, they bring forth fruit: thou art near in their mouth, and far from their reins (Jer. 12:1,2).

Likewise, thou, son of man, set thy face against the daughters of thy people, which prophesy out of their own heart; and prophesy thou against them,

And say, Thus saith the Lord God; woe to the women that sew pillows to all arm-holes, and make kerchiefs upon the head of every stature to hunt on souls! Will ye hunt the souls of my people, and will ye save the souls alive that come unto you?

And will ye pollute me among my people for handfuls of barley and for pieces of bread, to slay the souls that should not die, and to save the souls alive that should not live, by your lying to my people that hear your lies?

Wherefore thus saith the Lord God; Behold, I am against your pillows, wherewith ye there hunt the souls to make them fly, and I will tear them from your arms, and will let the souls go, even the souls that ye hunt to make them fly.

Your kerchiefs also will I tear, and deliver my people out of your hand, and they shall be no more in your hand to be hunted and ye shall know that I am the Lord.

Because with lies ye have made the heart of the righteous sad, whom I have not made sad; and strengthened the hands of the wicked, that he should not return from his wicked way, by promising him life:

Therefore ye shall see no more vanity, nor divine divinations; for I will deliver my people out of your hand and ye shall know that I am the Lord (Ezeo/13:17-23).

Mostly the younger mothers are the misguided ones. 'Funky and mod and cool' they are—and always have the quick, right answers. They form the direct opposite of mother Sarah's knees where Isaac was raised and trained. Young mums spout flawed wisdom to their children without the faintest knowledge or experience of the reality of the unseen world. With ploy of words they cast veils on the people with whom they associate. (*groot en klein, 1933 Afr. Version*).

Are only fortune-tellers guilty of (deliberately) applying falsehood to influence or drug receptive minds? It is the daughters of our good, honest, uninformed Christian folk who are the most careless and thoughtless with their idle chattering. Indeed, they are to be blamed for beguiling the credulous: 'Isn't this great fun!' With their idolatrous affinities as backing, they literally spin a disarming but soul-catching web with fantasies and dangerous imagery. Woe to their gullible babes; caught and enmeshed. Satan is quick to incite the most vicious and apparently innocent stories and programs for pre-school ages, and outrageously seizes territory in every age group without God-inspired authority effectively checking his advance in and through the Name of Jesus. Percentage-wise, Christians holding ground is in minority, yet, we but think God is asleep. *The waters compassed me about, even to the soul; the depth closed me round about, the weeds were wrapped about my head. (Ps.69:1, Lam.3:54, Jonah 2:51).*

The Subtleties of Self-life

During my early teens I witnessed a most interesting incident. and I have treasured the objective lesson ever since. Not only has it held me fascinated, but also as gullible, young and inexperienced in matters of the spirit and soul as I then was, could I detect the danger of self-life being transmitted from one person to another. Had I but given the matter serious and decisive prominence!

Today I marvel at how unobtrusively yet effectively the Holy Spirit supersedes when He sows His seed, for this particular incident was the initial shakings of my awareness, yet I slumbered on!

My Aunt Lizzie was visiting in our home when Megan and her three-year-old daughter came by for a cup of tea. We were seated at the dining room table when the restless child knocked her cheek rather severely against the corner, upon which Megan sharply slapped the table several times, repeatedly and vehemently scolding it: 'Naughty, naughty table, how dare you hurt the little girlie!' The crying subsided and the mother continued: 'Never mind, my darling, it isn't your fault, the naughty table won't do it again!'

The immediate response of Auntie Liz was equally enlightening. She lifted the child's hand in her own and with it stroked the offending table corner, quietly murmuring: 'Oh you poor, poor table, you can't talk and you can't tell me you are also hurting. Next time I will look where I am going. Sorry, table!'

Had I but given sufficient heed!

All begins with the self—self-preservation, prominence, comfort, convenience, possessions, justification, exoneration, gluttony, and enjoyment. The subtleties of self-life begin with self-deception.

How is it inculcated?

The serpent feeds it from day one in the mother's milk of Mrs. I-Me-Mine. Already with weaning, Self shows remarkable taste for sustenance of its own choice—or it won't eat. Sorry mum, even if healthy, nutritious food is set before it disguised by shape, size, colour and taste—unless sound, reasonable training commences with the first breath, you will have missed the boat.

Individual preferences get precedence—it will not tolerate any form of fasting or discipline. It will not concede nor submit, it is by nature rebellious, it will not give up the ghost and die. And bring my processed goodies, mom, I want to be fed, and I want it now! Any argument I can think of will do to serve selfish purposes for I can then toy with the grey areas and say 'How exciting! Great! I'm hungry, what's next on the menu? Let me have it now, and I won't wait!'

Sorry again, mum, fine-tuning is a difficult job, but it can also be overdone.

Self-deceit invents ways to feed self-indulgence. A carnal mother's children are her private seedling bed and, to gratify her ambitions, she will advertise what she has cultivated. The mentality propagating three-year-old Beauty Princesses will promote their product on-stage under glaring spotlights with flashing cameras and proud mamma will make sure the captions in the most widely distributed daily reads: 'A promising and brilliant future for an early career as the youngest Miss Space ever.' The best bit follows: 'She is the daughter of Mr. and Mrs. I-Me-Mine.'

The grey area ladder is cunningly constructed—hardly anything is left for the discerning not to say 'no-go, not acceptable'—and not much is left for our younger people in which to participate. Sunday School outings and hip-swaying praise-and-worship bands are susceptible activities. Understand from *Ex.32* that full-scale idolatry (Religious Whoredom) comes riding on the back of the golden calf, and in the last days the whoredom is shrouded in ear-shattering volume. The Holy Spirit is gentle—so gentle that He withdraws completely when foolish flesh pretends He has touched the meeting on the wings of blaring sound. All of it under our noses, and yet so far from our olfactory senses! So very acceptable, so very good: 'But it's the church, mom! All of us will be there! How can so many be wrong, mom?' Scores of Christians are ensnared by apparently innocent pursuits, lured into indulgences that are not from the heart of God.

Mr. White Sands Volley Ball and Miss Legs. Mr. Muscles, Junior. Miss All-Over Suntan 2007 (Senior and Junior Class.) We say 'Good, clean competition is a must for every growing child' and forget the Scriptural injunction that everything pandering to Self leaves the Holy Spirit grieving and withdrawing like the gentleman He is.

Competitions of this nature are often considered too tame and insipid to mention, and does not even deserve being listed on the same page with 'really exciting stuff' and the only merit these questionable activities deserve is the stage it provides as 'a starter' before the 'Real Thing' is served.

If we do not know the manner of the Holy Spirit, we will not be able to differentiate between sound self-image building, and slow strangling of the inner man by corruption in the mother's milk. It is not possible to build soundness on harboured self-deception. Teach the child to be honest with himself and others horizontally and vertically with God—and his walk will take him with a clean slate out of every situation in which he may find himself. Parenting is a formidable privilege, a terrible and frightening responsibility.

God has two poles operating—heaven and hell. Our preaching takes on only Heaven, leaving us expectant if not slumbering in the hope of glory. Our preaching does not shake us into a fear of God and His wrath. And yet, we thank God because emphasis on His Grace never is lost, but serves to magnify His forgiving, everlasting love.

Rave and E, and Tick, and Heavy Metal—and the latest contraceptives you have so *meaningfully* discussed with your eleven-years old—'my mom used to be so archaic, I swore I'd keep up with my own kids, you know!'

Today the list has become hideously unmentionable and those who warn and remonstrate against the unmentionable are found to be as offensive to those who participate in, and propagate the unmentionable. See one sheep dash across the road and over the cliff; watch the rest go scrambling after. Herd instinct. I can bluff myself as much as I like, I can play a game of hide-and-seek with myself, I can avoid exposure of my rottenness—and my child and I are lost, forever. A grey area is where truth and error get close to meeting; and is a breeding pen for hidden agendas.

Questionable areas are entered unthinkingly: any manner of secular competitive activities start children on the rat race. Keep up with the Jones'. Socialise at all costs. Partying is a must. Just that tiny bit more flamboyant and intriguing. The small folk love something new and special, don't they, my dear? Even at the expense of a groaning credit card and a groaning husband.

Children demand entertainment, they consider it their due, and parents feel guilty if they cannot comply with goods that one Rand more expensive. They concede to shocking tantrums, and they cannot say NO and mean it. Grey areas and compromise work together, and compromising is nothing short of lack of honesty in the inner man. Furthermore, tantrums and insolence provokes one into mouthing destructive utterances. God picks up what we say, and from it He creates the fruit of our lips and therefore we cannot be careful enough, for God operates on firm principles. *(Is.57:19a, 45:7, Prov.18:21).* Frightening?

You ask me how I can be so 'harsh and blunt about do this, and don't that' and I answer without hesitation: I *know*, because I walked my personal, poignant journey in painful denial. My offspring suffered not only as children but also as young adults because of my ignorance, and immaturity and lack of self-confidence. Had I known then, I would have implored the Lord first of all to put a restraining order on my tongue.

Now at the age of eighty, and to my shame, I admit that their wounding and disenabling was needless and all because 'I never knew' that God's merciful succour and protection work on principles as sound and inviolable as does His wrath. The Scriptural injunction is clear—get to know His principles and get your life straightened out accordingly and without delay.

How often we read in the Holy Bible of God's warnings and invitations to us: "If My people will, then I will …"

However, juveniles are seldom trained to occupy themselves constructively without someone supplying easily come-by wherewithal and stimulation. Modern technology has become the only support system, having replaced the antiquated dummy in the mouth. Man (both genders by implication) constantly sucked his dummy as a baby. As a juvenile he chewed his gum; and as an adult he has not outgrown his need for sucking. His tongue must work incessantly for subconsciously he still craves to sooth his unidentified needs with a dummy. The scope of this statement includes smoking, at a price, of course. Wagging tongues are not curbed—name it ethos. Worldwide and in another sense, oral stimulation is libidinous, licentious. The power of the tongue is indeed underestimated.

Schemes to keep youngsters off the streets could turn out to be a method of gaining illegal entry to their minds, and unrelenting evil sometimes permeate the activities contrived to win souls for the Kingdom. Evil is rife and undiluted. Individuals are pressurized by group instinct, unable to recognize the malady as fear of the opinion of men. Arguments based on self-deception, runs on the line of 'everyone else does it, you see'. This reasoning is in essence the self-deceiving cry of souls captured in a universal satanic onslaught.

Uninformed mothers are prone to feeding their infants with 'innocent' witchcraft. Feeding bottles are filled not only with superstitions and imagery, but also the unidentified ideals and hang-ups of the parents. Flights of the imagination are sparked off and fed by undiluted trash incessantly injected into the subconscious through the five senses.

Our world is loaded with adult females, odious to the extreme, bedfellows of the spirit of rape, who aid and abet their male counterparts in every depraved activity conceivable. These evil people are known to gain gradual, subtle, intentional and dangerous entrance into the privacy of homes and the relationship of child and parents. Their ultimate goal is total destruction of social Christian standards and values.

Never Too Late

It may appear that the previous pages have given evil too much prominence, but facts gained from daily events indicate the necessity for common-sense reasoning. If I am willing to observe globally, then I am also challenged to narrow the circle until faced with evidence in my own home and my own life. Never too late—as mothers we can stem the evil tide if we sterilize both bottle and milk.

We learn from Sarah to start cleansing our personal tents—to start where we are, use what we have, and let our babies suckle of the Word. If I succumb to the common malady of restricting personal assertiveness by thinking I am helpless and hopelessly inadequate to start changing matters in my home, then I suddenly discover God is the strong, faithful One who moves into the sphere of my desperation on the wings of ardent petition.

Everything we touch is tainted with the fever of restless, superficial busy-ness and leaves us with no time to ponder on the Word telling us that those who are dirty will become filthy. Those who are clean will be purified, and the holy ones will become even more holy *(Rev.22:11.)*

Adequate words cannot be found to describe the mess we have made of our beautiful world, and the small ones entrusted to our care. It does not take much imagination to think of the desperation of a small, live girl crudely desensitised, think of the wordless terror of a battered baby, of a fragile elderly woman raped, of the stunned emotions of a mother continually bearing assault for the sake of her young children, the shock of becoming an unfair victim of HIV, the horror-filled senselessness of war, the depravities inflicted on human and animal victims.

What man thinks the Word is saying is a far cry from what God is really saying! Every account of a supernatural occurrence in the Bible conveys with it the obvious—God is never without succour. He is telling us that He is Reality and yet keenly aware of each and every individual and incident ... telling us that He is more than willing to meet with each one of us on his or her level of understanding. God wants to be busy with ME, whoever I am. But only if I will let Him. Amazing! All I need do is to invite Him, mean it when I do, and let Him really take over!

And, behold, a certain lawyer stood up and tempted him, saying, Master, what shall I do to inherit eternal life?(Luk.10:25). Lost, lost, lost. Perhaps this was the last and final moment of decision for Jesus, son of man ... This lawyer had heard it all and still asks: 'What, and how?' Everyone, well, most of us, hears and reads it all and still wants to know: 'What, and how?'

Jesus knew the futility of human strivings and knew He would have to buy us. His Blood was the purchase price. It is the proof of His ownership. We are His precious possession. It does not take much imagination to see Jesus, His love pouring forth, slightly shaking His head, looking up into a clear blue sky and talking to Himself: 'My Father knows this lawyer just does not have what it takes. And neither does that old woman who will one day be teaching about submission. No matter how much effort she puts in, she can never pull herself through into the Kingdom of everlasting Life. Nor can anyone else ever make it unless I, the Son, submit and go pick up My Cross. My Father will have to hold Me closely lest I faint'

PART FOUR

THE BRIDE

Awake, O north wind;
and come, thou south;
blow upon my garden, that
the spices thereof may
flow out
Let my beloved come into
his garden,
and eat his pleasant fruits

(Song of Solomon 4:16)

1

THE CHAPTER OF
THE CAMELS

A High Standard

The significance of Sarah does not begin with her person nor does it end with her death. Rather, mystery around her is intensified when we learn that her son Isaac took his bride Rebekah upon arrival into his mother Sarah's tent.

After Eve and Sarah, God brings the believer with leaps and bounds further along the Way when He brings Rebekah onto the scene.

Rebekah, young as she is, simply steps forward and gives the camels to drink. Deep spirituality ...

The invisible Church is beginning to understand what the Almighty One had in mind when He depicted a Bride for The Man—her *spirit* must be suitable, adapted, and completing—and when her gown is without blemish, spot or wrinkle, (any such thing), the Father will bring her to His Son for the marriage supper *(Eph.5:27, Rev.19:7,8)*.

But now, will she be willing to leave everything and go?

He had made His Eve perfect, and she had disappointed Him. Then He exercised endless patience in His shaping of Sarah before she was anywhere near ready to begin the enormous task He had in mind for the eventual restoration of *Woman*.

Rebekah unpretentiously and graciously proffered drinking water and for the spiritual observer this is a powerful thrust of enlightenment from the Holy Ghost. With unwavering conviction she said 'I WILL GO!' And then, adorned with precious gifts of gold from his father's house, the camels brought her unto the man ...

The time has come to make adjustments to old and established conclusions concerning the Father's level for the Bride of His Son. The true Church hungers for more of direct teaching and would do well to identify with Habakkuk. Adequate words fail to give spark and vitality to the urge that led this prophet to give written utterance of what had transpired between God and himself. We are given to understand how Almighty God can, and does deign to communicate directly and clearly with ordinary human beings.

The first verses each of *Habakkuk Chapters 1 and 2*: gives a quickening description of the inter-action between God and Habakkuk, and the play of words gives us a taste of rare wine. We want this kind of relationship with God—we want more of it—but are we prepared to pay for it?

Habakkuk had a way of preparing himself to hear from God (the burden which Habakkuk the prophet saw): 'I will in my thinking stand up on my post of observation and will settle myself on the tower of the fortress and will watch to see what He will say to me, and what answer I will make as His mouthpiece'

The waiting and watching, the seeing, the hearing and the talking work together, miraculously, at the same time, supernaturally, inwardly and from without

These passages reveal the tempered steel of the true prophet and the genuine intercessor. These ordinary yet peculiar people *desire* a high standard. They are hard on themselves. They are willing to pay ransom for the release of this privilege and know that severe purging and grave responsibility are the conditions of contract. In contrast, a pretender bride wants the gifts but is not prepared to water the camels.

Bearing the above passages in mind, Genesis 24 offers tremendous teaching and dishes us a frightening standard.

Abraham was adamant. He was very sure he fully understood God's requirements and was not prepared to compromise and settle for second best. He therefore gives his head servant explicit instructions concerning the woman that was to be brought into his house as bride for his heir, and it would behoove servants of God to hear what the Holy Spirit is saying to each personally as they examine the Chapter of the Camels.

Jeremiah shuddered when he was compelled to speak out; he could not deny direct commands, he could not ignore the Creator's burning, consuming fire in his innards *(Jer.20:7-9)*. In Gen.24 a young girl dared the wilderness to reach her new lord—to offer him nothing but her whole being in submission—

Quest Of The Holy Spirit

Eliezer, eldest servant, ruled over all his master Abraham possessed, and was made to swear by the Lord, the God of heaven and earth, that he would not take a wife for Isaac from the daughters of the heathen Canaanites. She would be acceptable only if she came from the same country and the same family as did Abraham. No other options were to be considered. The servant said to Abraham:

'But perhaps the woman will not be willing to come along after me to this country where you now reside. Must I take your son to the country you had left?'

And Abraham said to Eliezer, 'See to it that you do not take my son back there.'

Profound.

Are we not inclined to reduce Jesus to our own level of thinking and living? Do we not bend backwards to accommodate a more comfortable point of view and fit Him into our country to suit our conveniences and still debate agreeably in our gatherings about going all the way with Him?

And the servant took ten camels of the camels of his master, and departed; for all the goods of his master were in his hand: and he arose, and went to Mesopotamia, unto the city of Nahor

And he made his camels to kneel down without the city by a well of water at the time of the evening, even the time that women go out to draw water (Gen.24:10,11).

Ten camels and ten attributes of the Holy Spirit—the hallmarks of the Cross of Calvary—**and the bride of the Heir has to be of the same kind, or she does not qualify.**

Truth, always forging ahead, leads a train of nine qualities equal in rank.

	separated-ness	surrender	commitment
Truth	obedience	sacrifice	suffering
	chaste-ness	hidden-ness	prayer

Eliezer prayed into the heart of God (long before Gideon enthrals us with similar exchange and audacity in *Judges 6,7)* and he gets results before he has even stopped praying:

'Please Father God, you choose, you send; let the right girl for the house of my master come to me and gives of herself willingly. You know what it takes for her to be found suitable, adaptable, completing. You know what the qualities are that will carry her to Him. You know what it will cost her to separate herself and leave her former life, her country, her relatives, her loved ones, everything that is familiar and dear, and take on a totally new committed life.

God, only you know if she is going to be found willing to mount my ten camels of testing and cross foreign country. Even if she does not resist the movement of these desert beasts of burden but abandon herself, resting on them, she will still be hot, shaken and tiring.

If she does come, then she is in fact, presenting her spirit, soul and body as a living sacrifice to her Bridegroom. She will no longer belong to herself or her people. She will not have any rights of her own. She will have to separate herself from her former conversation and style of life.

If she accepts the gifts of gold and silver, she will be Divinely inspired to **obedience and submission of a totally different quality than her present world knows of.**

Lord God, I have taken an oath; I have committed myself and am therefore held accountable for her until she is established in the tent of Isaac's mother. Father, I know that should she say: 'I will go!' and thus declare herself, she will bear the same name as the Bridegroom, and the same Life that is His, will also be hers.

The love that He personifies, will also flood her whole being and the sufferings and humiliations, rejection and persecution, being cast outside the city walls, the ruling and the reigning and the sharing of His secrets and His Kingdom, will also be hers ... her spirit will blend with His Spirit and His flesh.

The woman whom You send out of the city and her father's house, she will love me with the kind of love that shares Your Living Water with me ... within the clamouring city there is no pure water and also my camels thirst. They are kneeling, waiting to drink and be fed. She will have to care about them if they are to carry her all the way to the Eternal Bridegroom!'

Such Is Love

Before he had done speaking, lo, out came Rebekah, of the same family as Abraham, with her water jar on her shoulder. And the girl was very beautiful and attractive, chaste and modest and unmarried. And she went down to the well, filled her water jar and came up. And the servant ran to meet her and said, pray, let me drink a little water from your water jar. And she said, Drink, my lord, and she quickly let down her jar on her hand, and gave him a drink. When she had given him a drink, She said, I would draw water for your camels also, until they finish drinking *(Gen.24:15-20)*.

The head servant was in constant prayer: he gave truthful testimony; and his primary concern was a successful mission. His master should have no reason for either rebuke, disappointment or any regrets. Eliezer was totally reliant on the God of Israel to undertake and complete the quest for the right girl, but still the decisive question was: would she really relinquish ALL, forsake the familiar and replace it with a life held and owned by one other Man?

This is manna to the hungry. This is a breathtaking account of the work of the Spirit of God. Eliezer represents the Holy Spirit tirelessly at work, on mission, travelling across the deserts of the world. His quest is a Bride for the Heir, the only begotten Son of God.

The Holy Spirit is the only one who can protect her and bring her safely into Sarah's tent. But first he has to deal with all restraining bonds ... her family suggested she should go a little later on ... not now, not so soon, oh, anything just to keep her a little longer in their midst, in their little world ... just a few days later, perhaps? Perchance she herself may feel inclined to delay a final decision? But the servant said to the girl's family:

'Do not hinder and delay me ... I will not tarry but continue my search elsewhere!'

And Rebekah said: 'I WILL GO!' Decisively, emphatically. She put on the gifts of gold and joined the camel train that would take her into an entirely new life. She knew Eliezer would bring her safely to her waiting husband.

Rebekah could believe the Head Servant because he bore nothing but truthful witness: there were no doubts and no compromise, nor any wavering in his approach. His whole demeanour held stature and inspired Rebekah's trust. She knew he was speaking the Truth. In her heart of hearts she knew it was a call on her life, and she publicly committed herself to follow the servant and become The Bride. She had made a life-shattering decision. Obedience to a Person she had never seen in person, but who saw her—a Bridegroom from the Well of *One-Who-Sees-Me (:62)*

Eliezer was a praying man. His deference is all too obvious and we cannot but compare our ways with his for he never draws attention to himself. Such is the Holy Spirit—He ever works towards exalting the Father and His Son. *Howbeit when he, the Spirit of truth is come, he will guide you into all truth: for he shall not speak of himself, but whatever he shall hear, that shall he speak: and he will shew you things to come (Joh.16:13).*

It was essential for the bride to be chaste: pure, immaculate, spotless, virginal, unblemished. She would have to give of herself—without expecting anything back for herself—such is Calvary, and such is love.

Rebekah was relinquishing all her rights. Only reciprocating love could accomplish this. She needed learn to draw the fine line between negative, subservient passivity, and having her Husband conduct His Life-giving business through her own life.

This thing called submission would take on breathtaking shape and dimension; **it would also take infinite care of her self.**

Sacrifice and suffering go hand in hand; they are yoke-fellows and cannot be separated. There is suffering in laying aside the demands of a clamorous self-life, and much suffering in being weighed down with the gifts of gold and silver, symbolic of the Divine and the Redemptive work of Jesus Christ.

Rebekah would learn that if the suffering is spiritual, then there is also extensive physical depletion when identifying with a sick, angry and hungry world in prayer and practical service. She would never stop learning that having a servant-heart is a state of being and fruitless if attempted in the flesh.

This is not only awkward separation between the old ways and another Life for a new bride, but a true Bride closely associated with ten spiritual camels will also find intercessory desolation gnawing continuously at the heart of her empathy. Secularly and physically, the camels prove the point: they were waiting, kneeling beside a well, yet unable to drink without help; they were hungry and without fodder, unless it was provided.

2

WEDDING GUESTS

Co-Travellers

But to go a few steps further—these very camels had some of Abraham's men travelling with the head servant in his search. One would have thought they would demean themselves and do the necessary! They certainly did not! They sat back, all of them held by habit and steeped in custom, comfortably watching a female do the rough and the menial.

There cannot be any doubt that they knew what Eliezer's mission was, yet we do not read of their interested or eager participation in the head servant's request for God to propel His choice toward the well where the camels knelt. Little enough to expect genuine involvement, or even ask of them to pray ...

Nor do we get any information contrary to the final conclusion that they never became part of God's plan. They had ample opportunity of asking for drinking water from Rebekah's jar, because, although they enjoyed favourable amenities, (their feet were washed, their hunger met and thirst slaked in the home of the destined bride), they never made any meaningful contribution to the story above and beyond the fact that they may have represented safety in numbers travelling through a hostile world. If this is how believers spiritually read their presence in the general scheme of things, then what a delusion!

God is not interested in numbers but in quality!

We can safely assume that these men coming with Eliezer all the way, are those who tag along without any serious involvement or interest in the things of God. They are simply tick-picking birds feeding off the larger game, ready to rise in a flurry of flight at the least fanciful disturbance, settling down again on willing backs for the next fat pickings. Every congregation houses some such at the expense of tolerance and fellowship suppers and coke. And yet, they are Christians! We are exhorted to shed God's love abroad!

Their exposure to the unconscious aura of a Veiled Bride lies in the hands of the Holy Spirit only. If your leadership can identify these co-travellers as lazy, nit-picking criticizers stirring mischief and discontent, then get them, and the ticks, off the backs of your flock.

But now I have written unto you not to keep company, if any man that is called a brother be a fornicator, or covetous or an idolater, or a railer, or a drunkard, or an extortioner; with such an one not to eat.

For what have I to do to judge them also that are without do not ye judge them that are within?

But them that are without God judgeth. Therefore put away from among yourselves that wicked person.(1 Cor.5:11-13).

Harsh?

Scripture reads that the men who had travelled with Eliezer, also returned entourage to Abraham their master, with the prospective bride in their midst We immediately think of Christians who believe on Jesus as the Son of God, Saviour and Redeemer, and know that according to the Word they are saved, yet they will not sacrifice towards a life of committed excellence. They wait for someone else to water and feed the camels.

No Short Cuts

Coming with Eliezer all the way, some Christians miss out on all the important issues at the well and stand in danger of forfeiting a wedding dress of fine linen, gold and silver.

Let us be glad and rejoice and give honour to him: for the marriage of the Lamb is come, and his wife hath made herself ready.

And to her was granted that she should be arrayed in fine linen, clean and white: for the fine linen is the righteousness of saints.

And he saith to me, Write, Blessed are they which are called unto the marriage supper of the Lamb. And he saith to me, These are the true sayings of God (Rev.19:7-9)

Serious and dangerous questions may be asked, so take time on above three verses. Some teach that the church corporate (a body of individuals physically) is the bride. But here, however, the Bible teaches that it is the **righteousness** with which the Church-corporate has prepared and spiritually clad her self, which will be wedded to the Lamb. This **righteousness** is taken *from* the Church as Eve was taken *from* Adam, and Sarah is taken *from* the hole, pit, or well dug in the rock, Abraham *(Is.51:1,2)*.

Another group of saints, a great multitude in heaven, are rejoicing because the Bride has made herself ready (Rev.19).

Then also, there are blessed ones present who have been summoned to the marriage Supper. Who are these? We may feel ourselves safe as Christians and assume we can travel with the Bride, escort her, and ride into the heavenly feast with a guaranteed, reserved seat and place set ready, together with name card, without any arduous involvement whatsoever. But it won't jell when short cuts are attempted. A number of substantiating Scriptures prick the euphoria. *Mat.10:41, 1 Cor.3:8-15, 2 Cor.5:9,10* may be shot down, but take heed not to ignore the parable of the marriage supper told by Jesus in *Luke 14*. Only if clothed in the clean and white wedding garment of **righteousness** can presence at the wedding of the Lamb be ensured.

Jesus never made a redundant or irrelevant statement. He requested John the Baptist to baptize him and John promptly remonstrated, but Jesus replied:

*'Permit it just now, for this is the fitting way for (both of) us to **fulfil all righteousness—to perform completely whatever is right'** (Matt.3:13-15).*

Jesus again gives stringent instructions in *Matt.22:1-14* not to disregard the invitation to the wedding of the king's son and He clamps down mercilessly on guests who have gained entrance to the feast and taken a place without the appropriate wedding garments ... clean and white. *Then the king said to the attendants, Tie him hand and foot, and throw him into the darkness outside; there will be weeping and the grinding of teeth. For many are called (invited and summoned) but few chosen.* How all of it fits together is a mystery still to unfold; all we can do is to work at righteousness in our walk and talk, and steadfastly grow in faith while we await the Groom.

3

HE STEPPED FORWARD

And Isaac went out to meditate and in the field at the eventide, and he lifted up his eyes, and saw, and, behold.. the camels were coming.

And Rebekah lifted up her eyes, and when she saw Isaac, she lighted off the camel,

For she had said unto the servant, What man is this that walketh in the field to meet us? And the servant had said, it is my master: therefore she took a veil and covered herself.

And the servant told Isaac all things that he had done.

And Isaac brought her into his mother Sarah's tent, and took Rebekah, and she became his wife; and he loved her; and Isaac was comforted after his mother's death. (Gen.24:63-67).

4

THE WAY INTO AND THE PURPOSE OF

Interdependency

There were five, then four of us. Fellowshipping and interceding over many years, we would simply kneel down and get ourselves sorted out. With us there were no barriers; nothing hidden, confidences and trust never violated. No set time, getting together almost daily, each slipping quietly in or out as individual circumstances required. Praying, talking about the mysteries of God, treasuring the fragrance of His Holy Presence—how blessed we were!

We wept together, tasted and ate the Word, received deliverance, healing, and restoration. We learnt much, and with the Holy Spirit presiding and guiding, we grew. And so did sensitive awareness. We always knew when 'something' was 'happening' for one of us, and the shared wholesomeness was both joy and privilege, never taken for granted. The close circle was rare.

Marthina has a way of saying things: slowly, softly, sweetly, but with such firm conviction that it penetrates and lodges. Stuck. With the gift of wisdom and discernment moving on this particular occasion, she said only a few words about 'hidden components doing all the real work'.

It was a bull's eye. It hit home, straight. For me it was an 'Aha!' moment, an instant revelation, and my spirit soared.

In one second all of *1 Cor.11, 12 and 13* came to mind and fell perfectly into place. I was astounded. I had never seen this before, and neither have I, since the moment of insight, investigated other teachings in this area, nor have I looked back. Now, this is just exactly where my good friends Jeremiah and Habakkuk exhort me to boldness. Henceforth, 'I shall speak without fear what I see'. (Can my readers take it though, for I must of necessity be blunt)

The Secret Place of the Most High *(Ps.91:1)* is private and personal. It is the inner chamber or Sarah's tent, where the eternal Groom meets and fuses with His chosen bride. It is expedient for serious saints to find the **purpose of** and the **way into** Sarah's privacy.

Coupled saints must understand who they are in Christ, or the husband cannot successfully conduct or complete **the Lord's Life-giving business** through his sub-contributing wife, together in their tent. Each of the spouses must accept the responsible and accountable position-privilege and the power that is his, and hers, in Christ.

To reiterate: in the eyes of their Creator, a reborn couple, without losing individuality, autonomy and dignity, is considered as one.

What a husband and wife do for each other, they are doing as a service unto the Lord.

How they cherish each other in their daily lives and in spirit, determine the degree of spiritual consummation in their tent, the Secret Place of the Most High.

They will have come to a place of Godly love and life, and will bear Divine fruit accordingly.

To the few enlightened couples following the way together into Sarah's tent, to the presence of the waiting Bridegroom, is given the grace of experiencing the power of the Cross. Their life together has a cutting edge. They see the dead released, they see new life birthed.

They are fitting instruments for the Father's miracles.

Pulsing Through The Veins

As always, El Shaddai gives a vision—it is the manner in which He uses these married members, that beckons.

The pull with which the obedient couple is lured into a deeper experience of the Bridegroom becomes progressively stronger and clearer. The longing grows; it pulses strongly through the veins of their spiritual union and propels them to fusion with the Lord, beyond description. The desire to meet with the Son will not be stilled!

The real Bride is hidden from the eyes of the world—she veils herself until the moment of completion. She knows her sighs of petition and supplication have been heard. She will not be ignored by the only One who matters to her, but conceive. She will be satisfied and find herself resting in the strong arms of her Beloved. His peace will flood her being.

The Church, or Body, made up mostly of couples that function together in their tent in intercession on a level of purest righteousness, is a threat to Satan and it is obvious why marriages and families are the biggest target of his hatred.

1 Cor. 12:18-27

A tendency to spiritualise everything in the Bible does occasionally crop up and should be curbed, but it may, nevertheless, be edifying to take note of the interesting contents of verses 18–27.

No one can claim full conversance with any one, or all, of the supernatural endowments as set out by Paul. He is but skimming the surface and only as far as the Holy Spirit would have him go. He briefs on the diverse gifts functioning in the Church and enough only to serve several levels of growth. Of course he knew, and could write more, but chooses rather to move on and uses the human body as perfect illustration of the different members, the variety of functions, their interdependency, and action.

Consider then, briefly and in sequence, several verses but please remember that lateral literature contribute volumes: *for now we see through a glass, darkly, but then face to face: now I know in part; but then shall I know even as also I am known (1 Cor. 13:12).*

God perfectly chooses and places each of His gifted ones, and apportion to them. Paul exhorts us to *earnestly desire and cultivate the spiritual endowments (14:1).* We are to remain aware of our frail clay pots and that of ourselves we can produce nothing good.

:11,18. Individuals can be restricted by their utterances. Would it not be better if saints make no attempt to classify themselves, or make emphatic statements that 'I have the gift of ...'? Be willing to leave the operation of gifts in any given situation to flow through whomever the Holy Spirit chooses to use at the time—*just as He wished and saw fit and with the best adaptation.* Obedience to His voice calling the believer into action should be the major concern, and then the blessing will permeate the whole Body.

:12-19. But if the whole were all a single organ, where would the body be? Diversity has been the subject of much debate and dispute. Have there not been instances where the individuality of members (to cover the whole spectrum—from the timid to the brash) has been damaged by premature repudiation of their spiritual contribution toward the welfare of the body? *Gal, 6:6* can be quoted as yardstick: *Let him that is taught in the word communicate unto him that teacheth in all good things* This is not physical and material support only.

12:21. Unity, caring, sharing, esprit de corps. Do not be too quick in leaving your fellowship or cell if you detect a sense of dis-ease within yourself concerning the group. Examine your real motives before you look around for someone to support your observations and conclusions, and refrain from comment.

You may have scrutinized or possibly attempted an assessment of your stage of growth, and by now you know it is only honest and in-depth self-searching the Holy Spirit will use to lift you out of unrest, yet you may well be right in your perceptions of the external problem. The welfare of the group has priority however, and your dis-ease of spirit is secondary. Always the Light will penetrate and the Truth will set free. Why not rather nurse the group? Do this at the expense of your own feelings and face the possibility of losing face. Jesus will accept crucifixion of your self-life. He will sort out the rest of the Body and experience has taught that this might well happen, even to the latter's consternation and embarrassment!

12:22. Supposedly weaker parts and their contribution to over-all well being of the physique is taken for granted—until malfunction of the body draws attention to its discomfort and retardation. Paul had found the value of being weak. How the man must have been turned inside out! He thought, wrote, and walked with a thorough understanding of the power unleashed when a man is free of himself and weak in the eyes of the world.

11 Cor.12:7-10 uncovers his standard of surrender and total commitment—ever so difficult for any of us to emulate, much less maintain! *Therefore I take pleasure in infirmities, in reproaches in necessities, in persecutions, in distresses for Christ's sake: for when I am weak, then am I strong.*

There are couples, united in spirit, who attain to this level, but one does not hear of them; indeed, their travail and victories remain undisclosed. The more they are weak, free of themselves, emptied out, the more they receive His fullness, the more they have power with God and man, the more purpose they have in their mission, the less they seek acknowledgement.

1 Cor.12:23 Considered by some ignoble, unimportant, unseemly? Weak, hidden, covered? Through them the Lord conducts His Life-giving business—drainage and reproduction. Hidden components doing all the real work? *'Aha!'*

In this verse the hidden-ness of purposeful, single-minded intercessors are summed up to perfection. The Bride removes her veil only in the privacy of her tent. *Nothing* comes between this kneeling couple and the Eternal Groom. *Nothing* should impair their relationship. Discretion is a key factor: intercourse and elimination are never discussed. The intercessor is too cautious and will never disclose private details concerning the hard work of prayer.

These two functions are indispensable services rendered to the Body and express the most vital of all the **sub**-roles contributing to the **mission** of the Church.

Reproduction of the human species has lost prominence—the desire to add another baby to the family is outdated. 'They happen by accident'. Licentious activities are justified by placing emphases on for instance poor economic conditions, or financial stress. Present-day reasoning promotes promiscuity—it sells just about everything on the market. A twisted concept of sex has deliberately been cultivated and sold to both susceptible genders.

Private organs connect only with the sexual act and perverse thinking turns any personality into a stronghold of driving sexual needs demanding unacceptable expression. One has rights, does one not? Enjoy instincts and live fully and freely, why not? After all, the 'government and the people' (taxpayers) cannot afford to run institutions for suppressed and stunted psyches! There should be no restrictions!

Physical drainage and elimination, considered unmentionable (but not as crude expletive habitual to many), understandably takes an ignoble place. This healthy, daily function is taken for granted—so much so that we read about weak, private parts in three verses and never reserve time or space for contemplation or meaningful debate. And this is where we reduce Paul's intended (?) message to an underestimation of its value. The contribution *22,23 and 24* makes to our understanding of the ministry of intercession should actually be nudging our thinking into first gear.

Hidden components are defenceless, spiritually and physically, unless thoroughly covered. The Lord knows how vulnerable His Bride is without His protection and personal care. Her righteousness (the key to His kingdom) is very precious to Him. Abraham conveniently forgot this, and Adam did not seem to know or care … The Evil One blatantly attacks all righteousness and he has deliberately chosen to reduce private affairs to smutty discussion, obscene advertisement and public viewing. Gross indecency is no longer rebuked as unacceptable and Christians appear to have become tolerant of the unhealthy climate.

In direct contrast, the singles, and married couples who quietly and righteously walk the Way, do not appear strong or regarded as important to the rest of us because they work for the Kingdom and the Body without show, acclaim, exposure or public recognition. This is a paradox and how the Devil would twist if it he but could! The veiled Bride is doing all the hidden work: she is available and used of God in a place where she does not permit any fleshly intrusion. In her yielding weakness lies His accomplishing strength.

These unobtrusive and humble ones are sustained and maintained by God. He works through His gifts, so exquisitely balanced in a prepared Body, who should be knowledgeable enough to protect the spiritual privacy of intercessors with their anointed mantle. And, yes! We know **the standard we are seeking is high, and very costly ...**

1 Cor.12:24 shake us a bit. Our Lord is not impressed with adulation of prominent, successful, distinguished, lime-lighted Christians. He uses them mightily, but according to this verse the attractive, more presentable parts of the body do not require being treated with the same deference as the less comely, hidden parts, for which the world has no esteem. With the least taint of self, some dynamic authors, cell-leaders, breath-taking preachers and eye-catching televangelists, may have minimized their share of reward. Toughies. They are not veiled but go about openly with round figure donations, adulation, headlines, advertisement, and canvass with soul-winning publicity. The public are inclined to fan mail and go overboard in hero-worship, and the inference here is that any kind of platform, be it pulpit or public performance, sells your form according to your performance. Careful. The snake comes slithering in without a hiss and before long idolatry raises its head to strike and how deadly is the venom of pride mixed with religion! Jesus spoke firmly in *Mat.23:5-8*.

If a person is not called and anointed by God to fill a prominent or any particular position in the Church, yet holds it, then he is toying dangerously with the soul of the Body. I may not, without God's anointing, take charge of a position I cannot handle judiciously, and I will be accountable for dry and dead results.

In the final analysis, the crux of 'covering' is the Person of Jesus: not a church, nor any other being. A saint who discerns where the need is for warfare, prayer and support of especially the intercessors, will directly enter the presence of our High Priest and find Him responding with supernatural succour *(Eph.3:19,20. Heb.7:24,25)*. The veil has been rent. We have entry! This sturdy saint though, will not endorse 'going it alone' nor go around yapping about what he knows is being accomplished behind the scenes. The work of the Spirit is sacred, and not to be dissipated by wayward-ness or wagging tongues and nosey parkers.

:26 speaks for itself, and *:27* boils down to this: I may not covet the position of a fellow saint, but am to strive rather for the spiritual endowments *(1 Cor.14:1,12)* and leave the person, place or position of another well alone. If I am not flooded with the love His Presence emanates, then I have not yet come to

the place of His rest. All my strivings in the flesh to be like someone else will in any case be futile, so why be jealous of gifts and talents?

If I genuinely enjoy being a kitchen maid and have discovered I have a flair for peeling potatoes at high speed like no one else you have ever seen, then I have a responsibility to my Creator not to be envious of my dear sister who is always evoking Maria Callas beside me in the praise-and-worship sessions. The painful difference between my neighbour's beautiful, trained warble and my own inharmonious croak serves an excellent purpose, for I am thus continually (and this is grace!) reminded of my even greater charge—I am to work out my salvation with fear and trembling for it is God working in me both to will and to do of His good pleasure. And this includes the potatoes and all carnal inclinations sure to come assailing a gift from God, be it physical or spiritual, my own or that of any other *(Phil.2:11,13)*.

So then every one of us shall give account of himself to God (Rom.14:12).

5

SARAH'S TENT

May I Address You Personally?

If you believe God has called you into holy wedlock, your solidarity as couple should be at the sole disposal of the Lord. There are no other options. You are called Sarah; you are endowed and gifted and charged to exert subjective influence on Isaac. You will find yourselves placed where God needs you. Failure to comply will earn failure in every other place you put your selves and may well become a forty-year journey through the wilderness with pretty severe trials until each lesson is learnt.

Should you be determined to mount the camels and have Eliezer lead you to the Bridegroom, Jesus will step forward and meet you when He sees the camels approaching. Veil yourselves. You will be taken into Sarah's tent where your life of burden bearing begins ...

Response to the call of God grows. Retiring together then in the inner chamber and have the Spirit woo you into spiritual consummation—these are the hours of which no one knows—totally dependent on Jesus to lead you into deeper depths—a sigh often accomplishing as much as heart rending intensity—the resurrection power of the Name and the Blood never disappointing, never depleted—completely sold out to Jesus, and His presence and good favour will be yours beyond human comprehension.

Together you will drain reborn members of the last dregs of lodged filth and muck. You will deal with the residue of sin in the lives of those the Spirit brings before you. With travail and agony the eliminatory process, the cleansing and the restoration are wrought. You will defuse every defect and flaw.

God's love is reciprocal; it works in and between each other and God, it spills over to touch, bless and warm those in need of it. Divine inter-action increases with time and obedience.

Keep yourselves in all righteousness; be **hid in Christ.** Wearing the bridal gown is an honour—no recognition, no acclaim accompanies the commitment.

Your gown is nothing but a double portion of suffering and pain, and responsibility to foster the Lord's private business unto yourselves. Know that the fine white linen, spotless, without blemish, adorned with embroidery and precious stones, are obtained not only by good works and righteousness, but also by the sad joy of sacrificial love. This could include martyrdom. Few can take this testing.

Your voices will seldom be heard in the crowded gatherings. Weigh every word carefully.

Are you prepared to keep a low profile? Yes? Then often your personal interests will run second or last. This also means that you will not be lusting for attention or attainment. You will increasingly find you do not heed your flesh—then only does He begin to use you—and you would have entered a life unexplainable. You are to seek nothing but dying to self, nothing but Him.

A holy fusion takes place when you are of one mind, and this is the primary factor for the conception of new spiritual babes. The growth of God's family rests on your faith and robust stability.

You can work at your personal diversities from this point on—understanding, consideration, and the all-important communication. These are the areas in which you are most likely to be attacked or caught off-guard. About this you must make no mistake! It is your mate you have to protect first and foremost. Do not as the first Adam did, but as last Adam demonstrated—He died for His bride.

But, you will be a force to be reckoned with.

The enemy's target will be your unity because you are in the place together where the Holy Spirit plugs in to conceive a new work of God. You may find yourselves praying in strange places whilst on your knees. It could be the genuine repentance of a believer, or a mighty move of God in some pagan area; the Spirit knows no bounds. It may be revelation or prophecy. Whatever! God alone knows! And really, saints, it is none of our business what He plans. Your job is unquestioning obedience, and together!

Never is there to be any ferreting for information you think you could use in warfare. Satan will attempt to sidetrack with feeding truth-appearing lies and speed you on your way to defeat and damage. What you need to know for the purpose of specific prayer will be channelled through, and confirmed, in surprising and most unlikely ways; always a surprise and a delight. And, you clank your jaws shut to the rest of the fellowship and the outside world. Question your committed obedience if you do not suffer persecution for it. You will find yourselves walking supernaturally, but it calls for sacrifice, secrecy, self-discipline, humility and unity.

Don't ask for results, and certainly not according to your assessment or expectations. This is to restrict the Holy Spirit, because what we determine as results could be our own impoverished level of expectation or judgment. Even so, you may feel led to be very specific. There is no blue print for penetrating prayer.

Sometimes, when faced with a predicament, we ask for a sign, which certainly we may do, as much as the temptation is also there to take a lucky dip from the Bible. God delights to reveal Himself, but signs and wonders remain His prerogative. For Gideon it was necessary to put a fleece of wool on the threshing floor to make sure by sign that it was God's dealings, but I should say, if I may, that you are to deny yourselves the tendency to ask for signs at random. This is conducive to unbelief.

Radical faith is the natural habitat of signs and wonders, but bear in mind how the Serpent is ever present, coiled, raised, ready to strike and supplant with his own signs. Unfortunately, we are all prone to believe what we want to hear, act upon it, and the battle is lost before it is even begun, leaving a trail of destruction in it wake.

Never forget, Sarah, you have subjective spiritual influence upon mankind whether near or on the other side of the world.

To open the blind eyes, to bring out the prisoners from the prison, and them that sit in darkness out of the prison house.

But this is a people robbed and spoiled; they are all of them snared in holes, and they are hid in prison houses, they are for a prey, and none delivereth; for a spoil, and none saith, Restore.

Bring forth the blind people that have eyes, and the deaf that have ears (Is. 42:7,22, 43:8).

You have been espoused to one Husband (*11 Cor.11:2*). You have eaten of His flesh and drunk of His Blood and now you are consumed with desire for Him. God will divulge to a few only what impassions you so, but never advertise that you are Abraham and Sarah conceiving Israel.

Sure there'll be raised eyebrows in your circles because you're not flapping to go places and do good things. Of course, Satan will provoke some well-meaning Christian enthusiast to pester you into time-consuming works 'for the Lord, you know!' Get, and keep, your priorities straightened out.

Also remember this: the bigger the church, the easier to hide within numbers; less acute then the demand for costly love on a personal basis, and much easier to slide into external religious affairs with fetes and barbecues. All these activities beckon the serious saint as soothing substitutes for the intercessory call, beguiling and lulling the sense of urgency.

No!! Stick to the call on your life. Stay in your tent and stick to childbearing. You are to take a firm stand against usurpation of your faith, your time and loyalty. Sarah, Rebekah and Rachel had problems withholding them from conceiving. History informs that these women, and their husbands, needed to go through the scorching of God's purging: the cheating, the stealing and lying, the adultery and idolatry had to be dealt with till God was satisfied. Eventually they did conceive, yes, but we now are in the climate of Grace and this is the platform from which we are privileged to pray and seek His face in petition and supplication.

Faithfully persevere through those long, lonely, nine-month gestation periods if so engineered by the Lord. Eventually you will find yourselves shunted out by those very same numbers, ignored and overlooked. Praise God! You don't take yourselves out. You find yourselves put out. A noteworthy difference. Decide what you want—to be seen and heard of men, or as Jesus said: '*I have meat to eat that ye know not of*' *(Joh.4:32,34).*

It is the hidden components that do all the real work: carry the developing babe, together. Agonize, travail in pain till the birthing is completed. Let the Father charge the best suited saints to carry out the all-important nursery care—those who change and wash the dirty nappies by hand, till the newly-born no longer are fed with milk but can take the solid. You can be very sure Father not only provides, but also equips the nannies. You just step into the next job He brings to you: one of mind, one heart, one purpose. His will alone be done.

What is it God wants of us?

A man and his woman walking together in close and intimate communion with Him!

Abraham, submit your faith to your wife. Surrender your trust to her, FUSE with her in prayer. Take the lead and bring her into Sarah's Tent. Your mission is Life-giving—spiritual progeny reflecting the glory of our Father in Heaven.

Sarah, submit to the Jesus indwelling your Adam. He asks of you to conduct Divine influence on your husband. Do not discuss or draw attention to your sublime understanding of submission, but enter the rest of God. Your surrender, and commitment to do all as if unto the Groom, must be complete and, most certainly! Israel will be born unto your Lord

Thus we have the Christ-Bride: the righteous spirit of a man and his woman. And Father God brings her unto the Man, His only Begotten Son, the Heir Jesus Christ.

Oh yes! He is sure to come walking again in His Eden, in the cool of the day, and this time you will have no need of fig leaves. Nor will you be hiding in a shelter of lies. This time you will answer with a joyous love call—

HERE WE ARE, FATHER GOD,

HERE WE ARE!!

Fruit of Life!

AFTERWORD

It is true—the twelve disciples our Lord sent forth to teach His words were men only. Yet how overwhelmingly significant that Jesus, when He had risen, bypassed His inner circle of eleven and first appeared to Mary Magdalene and the women with her. To these faithful, watching, waiting, caring ones He revealed Himself fully, sending them off with the glorious message: **'Go, tell My brethren, I am the ascending Christ!'**

The four Gospels carry the same inference: these women were not taken seriously when they brought the message.

Luke 24:10,11 And their words seemed to them as idle tales, and they believed them not.

Mark16:14 Afterward He appeared unto the eleven as they sat at meat, and upbraided them with their unbelief and hardness of heart, because they believed not them which had seen Him after He was risen.

Man! As it was then, so it is today—women are not taken seriously.

On the final page I would like to share a vision with you, and whether you think *Jer. 31:22* in context here or not, I cannot tell, but the last words of the verse keep ringing in my mind: '… a *woman shall compass a man* …' (Compass meaning: a circumference, boundary, area, extent, protect, hem in, go round).

Indeed, indeed, for the backslidden wife this is a tremendous word, fresh and new does God do a wonderful thing for the restoration of mankind should Woman lay hold of the principle!

Set thee up waymarks, make the high heaps; set thine heart toward the highway, even the way which thou wentest: turn again, O virgin of Israel, turn again to these thy cities. How long wilt thou go about, O thou backsliding daughter? For the Lord hath created a new thing to the earth, A woman shall compass a man (Jer.31:21,22).

(Rig vir jou mylpale op, maak vir you padwysers, let op die grootpad, die pad wat jy geloop het. Kom terug, o jonkvrou van Israel, kom terug na hierdie stede van jou!

Hoe lank sal jy bly aarsel, o afkerige dogyter? Want die Here het iets nuts op die aarde geskape: Die vrou sal die man beskerm).

THE VISION

I was shown a dark, dense jungle, and a narrow footpath along which a family of five were cautiously winding their way in single file.

The man was forging ahead with nervous, wary steps, ready for instant action. He was keenly alert, spear poised in raised hand, his eyes searching the forest about, yet with never a glance over his shoulder backward.

His three youngsters were closely following him. Their ages, I should say, ranging five to ten. On their heels came the mother, her eyes fixed firmly on the back of her husband, never wavering. She was constantly watching his every move.

I gasped as I realized the implications. As I saw it, in any such dangerous territory, the enemy would always attack the rear first, and being last in line, she was unprotected and vulnerable. I cried out: "Lord! What are You showing me! The man won't even know until it's too late! Should she be targeted, darted and felled, the whole family could be taken down one by one! She's utterly exposed with her back left open and unguarded!"

And then came the beloved Voice: 'Shush, child! Not if she's totally mine and faithfully stays IN Me. Understand Me well, this little woman is clever enough to keep her back covered. She knows she is last in line and that gives her first claim on Me. I am the Almighty One—she keeps herself Christ-encased, and I cover her back!"

I sighed and was instantly at peace. I said, "Thank you, Father, I understand. Yes, I understand.'

978-0-595-44435-9
0-595-44435-0